NOV 2 1 2007

17

5/08
9/11

Discarded By Elk Grove
Village Public Library

D1528561

INVENTIONS AND DISCOVERY

FRANK ZAMBONI

and the Ice-Resurfacing Machine

by Kay Melchisedech Olson

illustrated by Richard Dominguez
and Charles Barnett III

Consultant:
Beth Davis, Curator
World Figure Skating Museum
Colorado Springs, Colorado

Capstone
press

Mankato, Minnesota

Graphic Library is published by Capstone Press,
151 Good Counsel Drive, P.O. Box 669, Mankato, Minnesota 56002.
www.capstonepress.com

Printed in the United States of America

1 2 3 4 5 6 12 11 10 09 08 07

Library of Congress Cataloging-in-Publication Data
Olson, Kay Melchisedech.
Frank Zamboni and the ice-resurfacing machine / by Kay Melchisedech Olson; illustrated by Richard Dominguez and Charles Barnett, III.
p. cm.—(Graphic library. Inventions and discovery)
Summary: "Describes how Frank Zamboni created the ice-resurfacing machine, and how it affected the world of ice-based sports"—Provided by publisher.
Includes bibliographical references and index.
ISBN–13: 978-1-4296-0147-4 (hardcover)
ISBN–10: 1-4296-0147-7 (hardcover)
1. Zamboni, Frank J., 1901–1988—Juvenile literature. 2. Inventors—United States—Biography—Juvenile literature. 3. Zambonis (Trademark)—Juvenile literature. 4. Skating rinks—Equipment and supplies—Juvenile literature. I. Dominguez, Richard. II. Barnett, Charles, III. III. Title.
GV852.O47 2008
688.7'691—dc22 2007000254

Designer
Bob Lentz

Production Designer
Kim Brown

Colorist
Melissa Kaercher

Editors
Christopher L. Harbo and Aaron Sautter

FRANK ZAMBONI and the ICE-RESURFACING MACHINE

TABLE OF CONTENTS

Chapter 1

BROTHERS IN BUSINESS

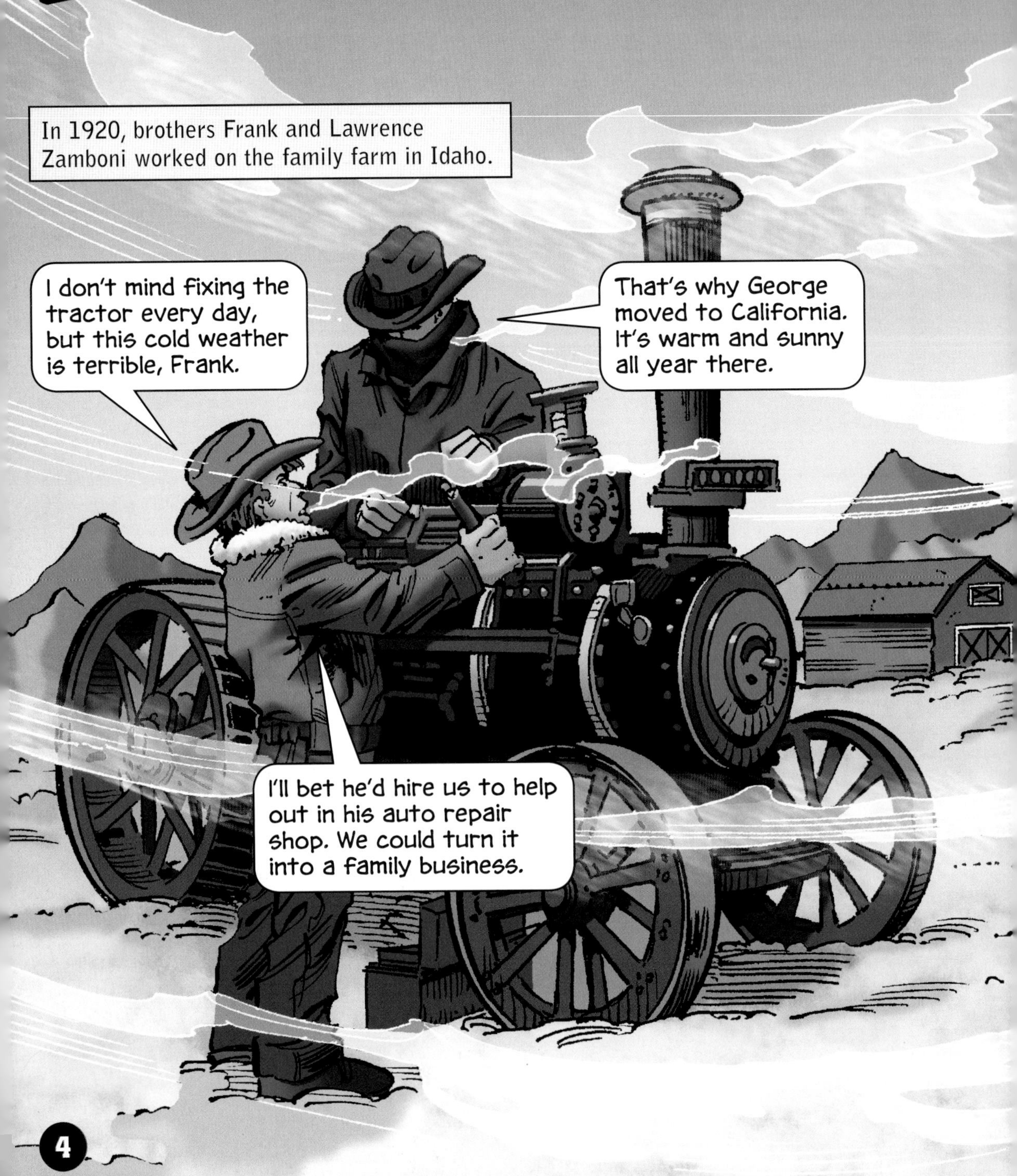
In 1920, brothers Frank and Lawrence Zamboni worked on the family farm in Idaho.
I don't mind fixing the tractor every day, but this cold weather is terrible, Frank.
That's why George moved to California. It's warm and sunny all year there.
I'll bet he'd hire us to help out in his auto repair shop. We could turn it into a family business.

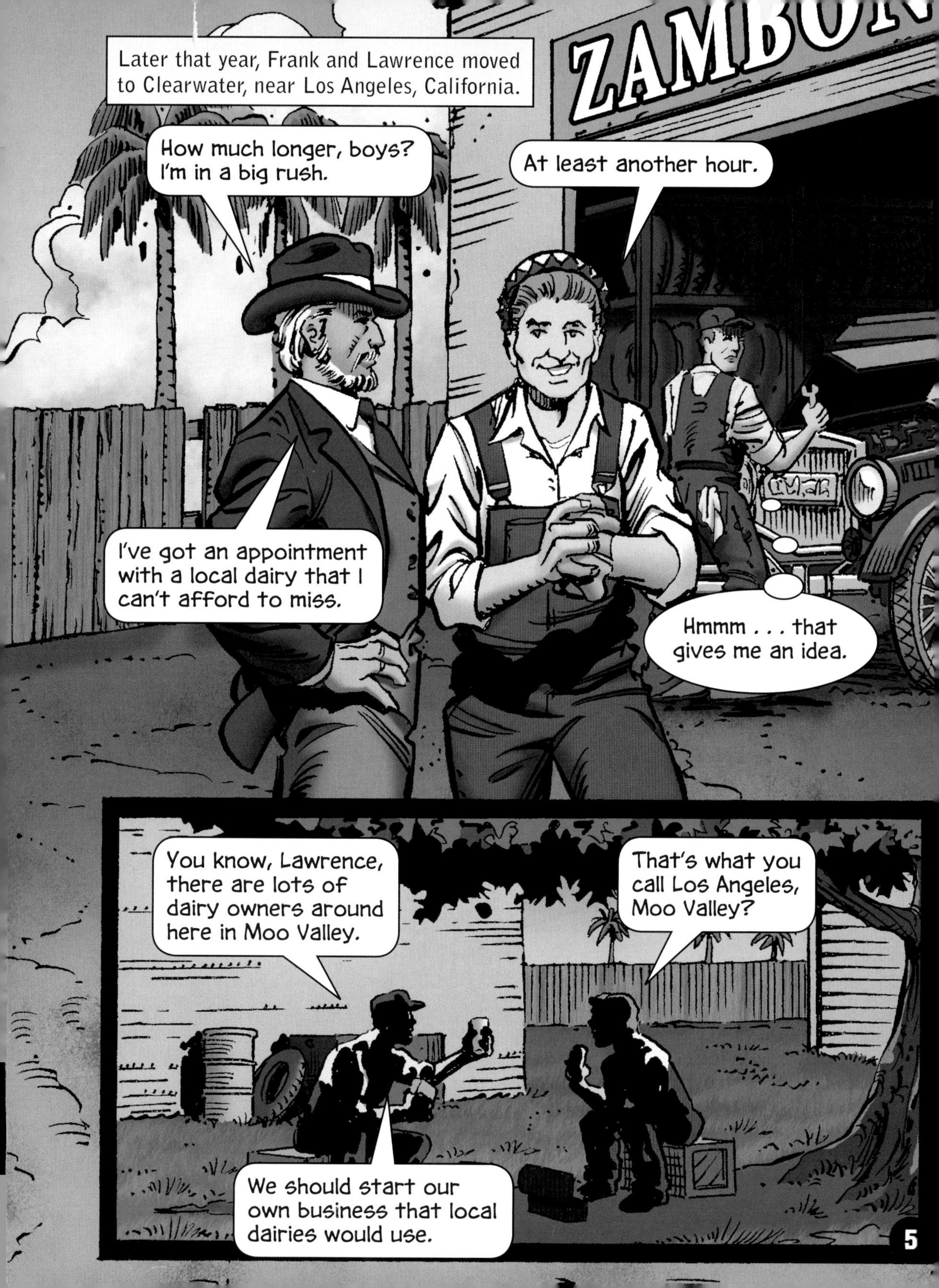
Later that year, Frank and Lawrence moved to Clearwater, near Los Angeles, California.
ZAMBON
How much longer, boys? I'm in a big rush.
At least another hour.
I've got an appointment with a local dairy that I can't afford to miss.
Hmmm . . . that gives me an idea.
You know, Lawrence, there are lots of dairy owners around here in Moo Valley.
That's what you call Los Angeles, Moo Valley?
We should start our own business that local dairies would use.

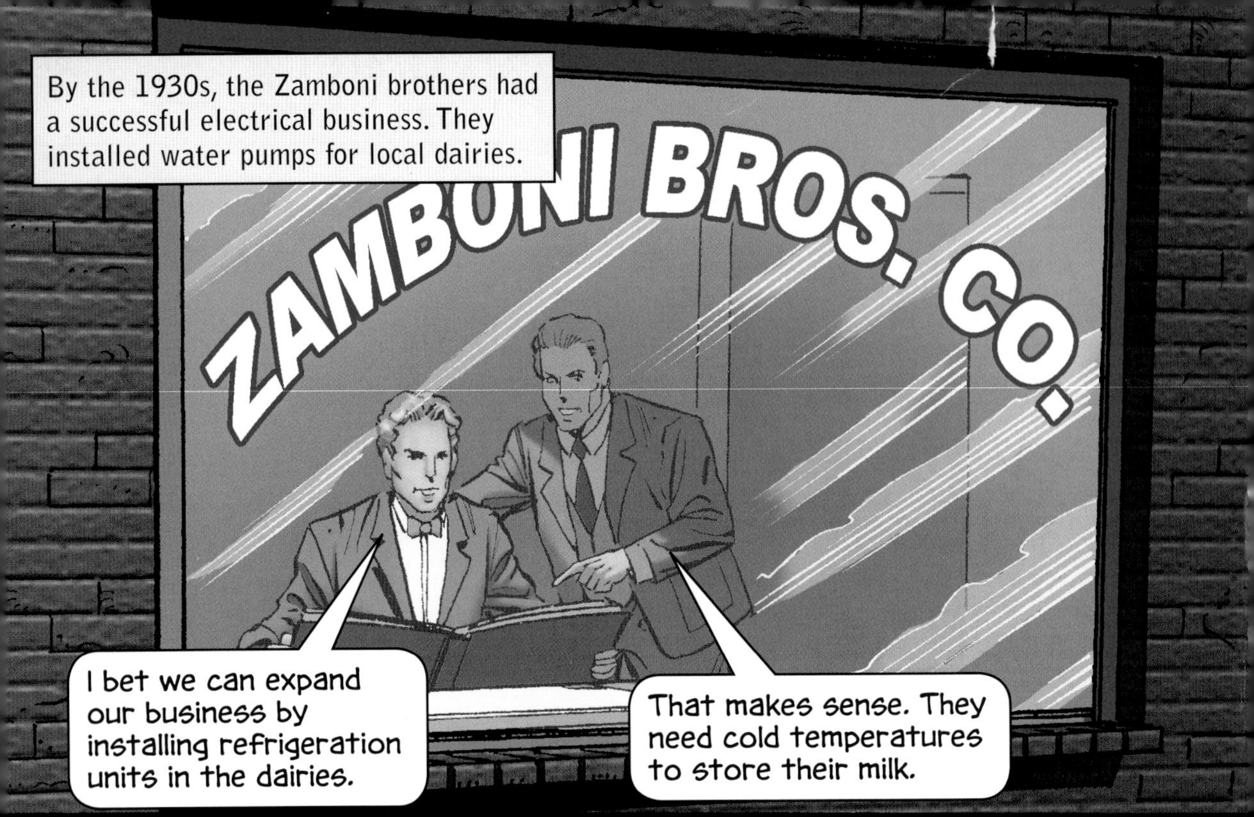
By the 1930s, the Zamboni brothers had a successful electrical business. They installed water pumps for local dairies.
ZAMBONI BROS. CO.
I bet we can expand our business by installing refrigeration units in the dairies.
That makes sense. They need cold temperatures to store their milk.

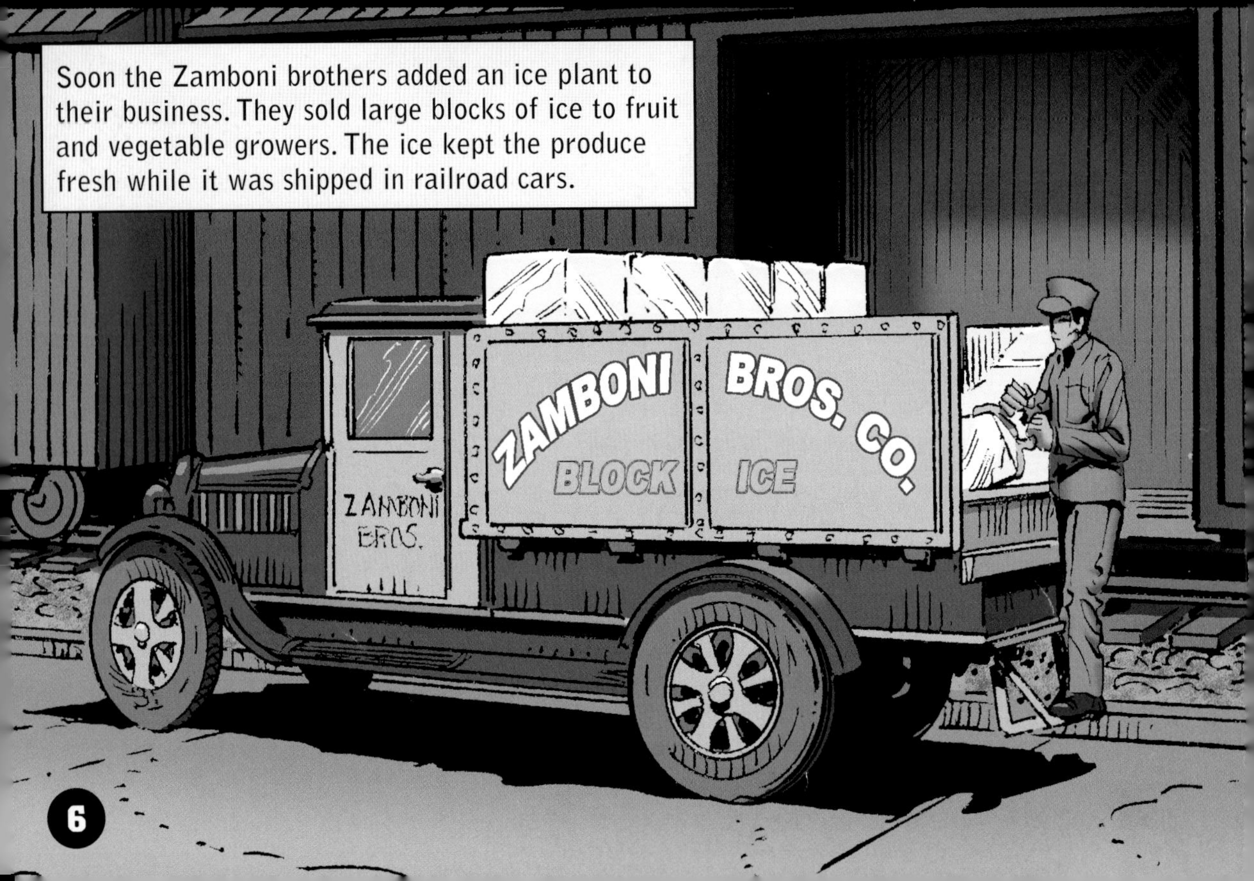
Soon the Zamboni brothers added an ice plant to their business. They sold large blocks of ice to fruit and vegetable growers. The ice kept the produce fresh while it was shipped in railroad cars.
ZAMBONI BROS. CO.
BLOCK ICE
ZAMBONI BROS.

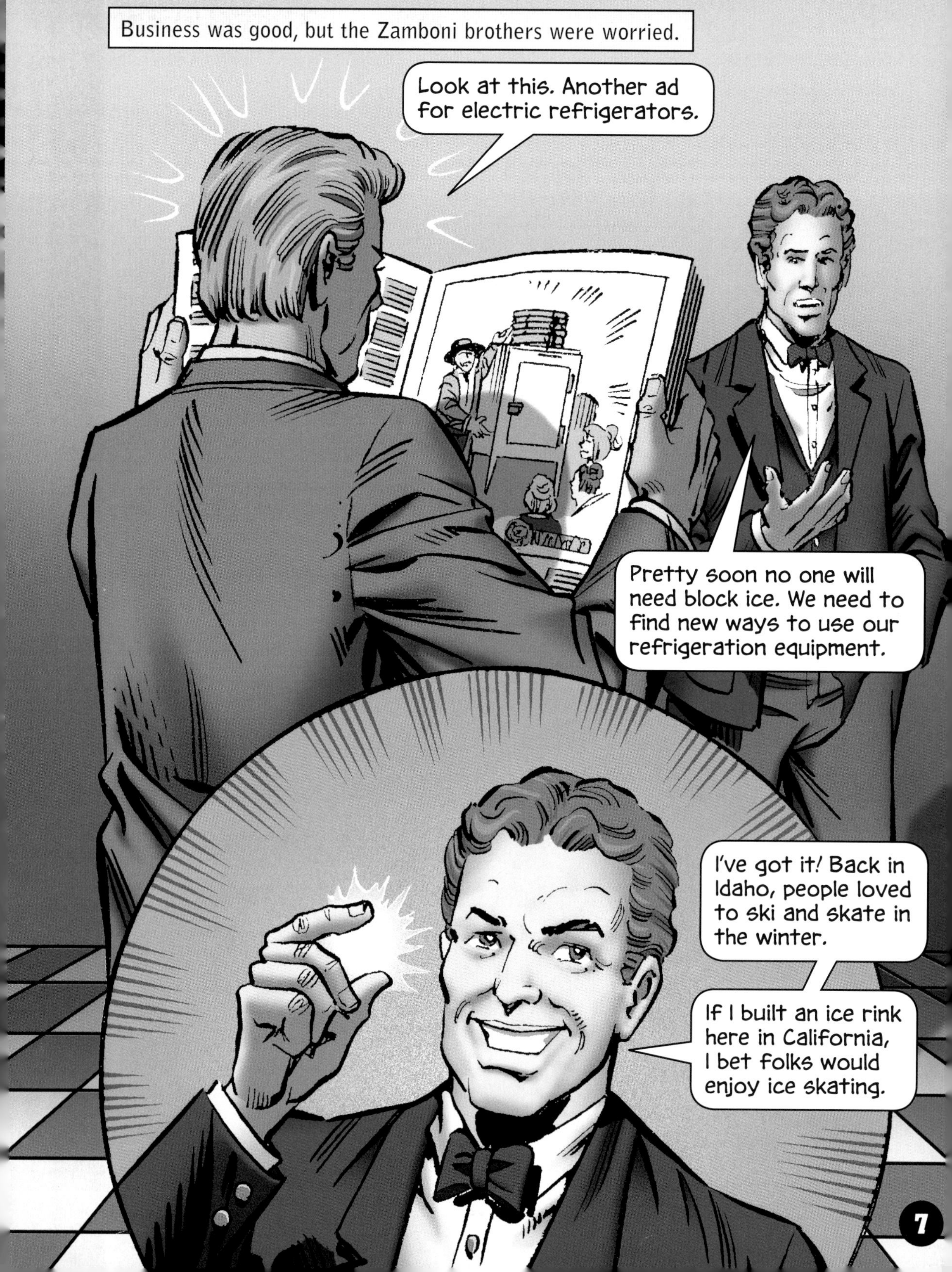

Business was good, but the Zamboni brothers were worried.
Look at this. Another ad for electric refrigerators.
Pretty soon no one will need block ice. We need to find new ways to use our refrigeration equipment.
I've got it! Back in Idaho, people loved to ski and skate in the winter.
If I built an ice rink here in California, I bet folks would enjoy ice skating.

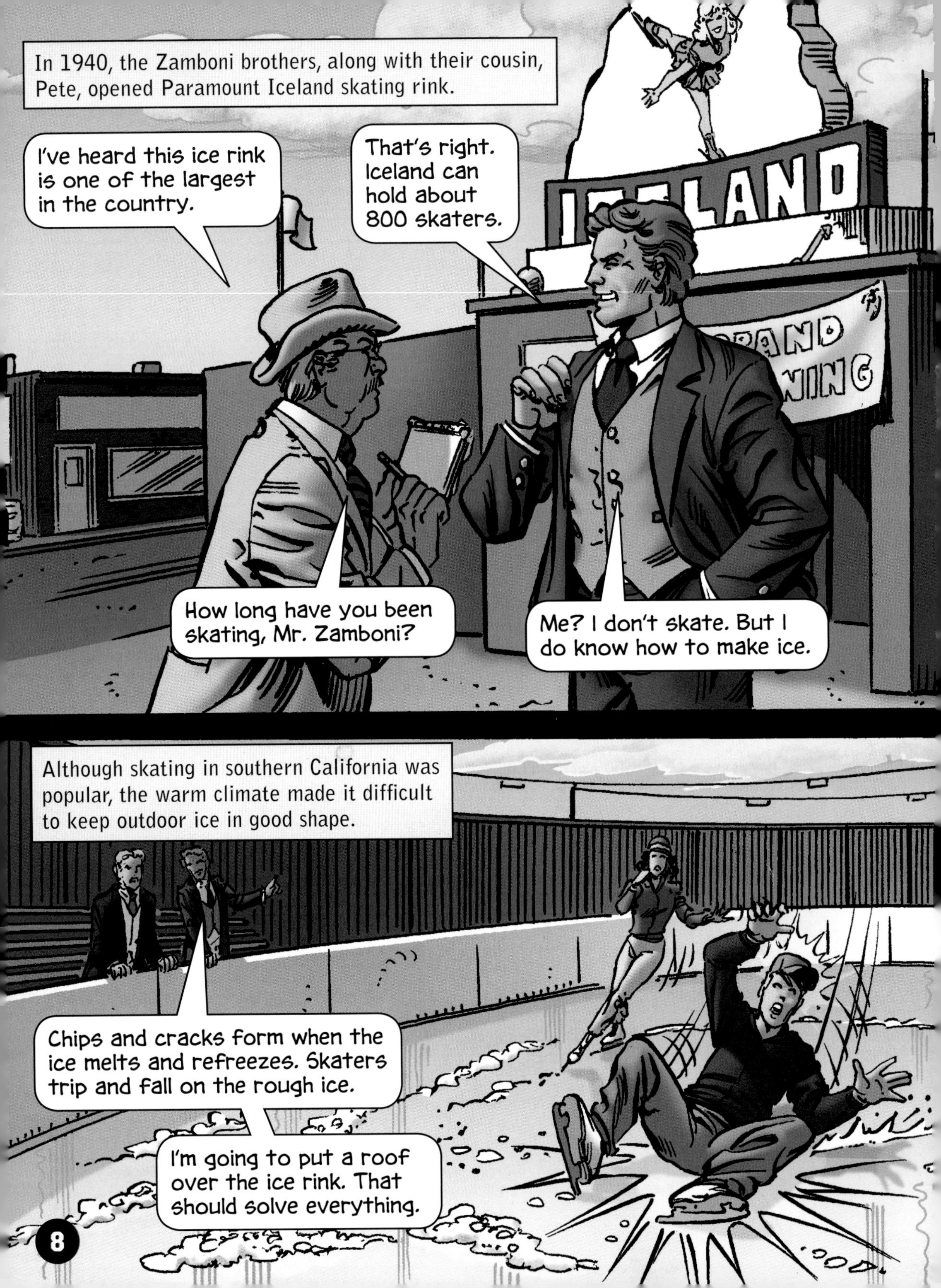
In 1940, the Zamboni brothers, along with their cousin, Pete, opened Paramount Iceland skating rink.
I've heard this ice rink is one of the largest in the country.
That's right. Iceland can hold about 800 skaters.
How long have you been skating, Mr. Zamboni?
Me? I don't skate. But I do know how to make ice.
Although skating in southern California was popular, the warm climate made it difficult to keep outdoor ice in good shape.
Chips and cracks form when the ice melts and refreezes. Skaters trip and fall on the rough ice.
I'm going to put a roof over the ice rink. That should solve everything.

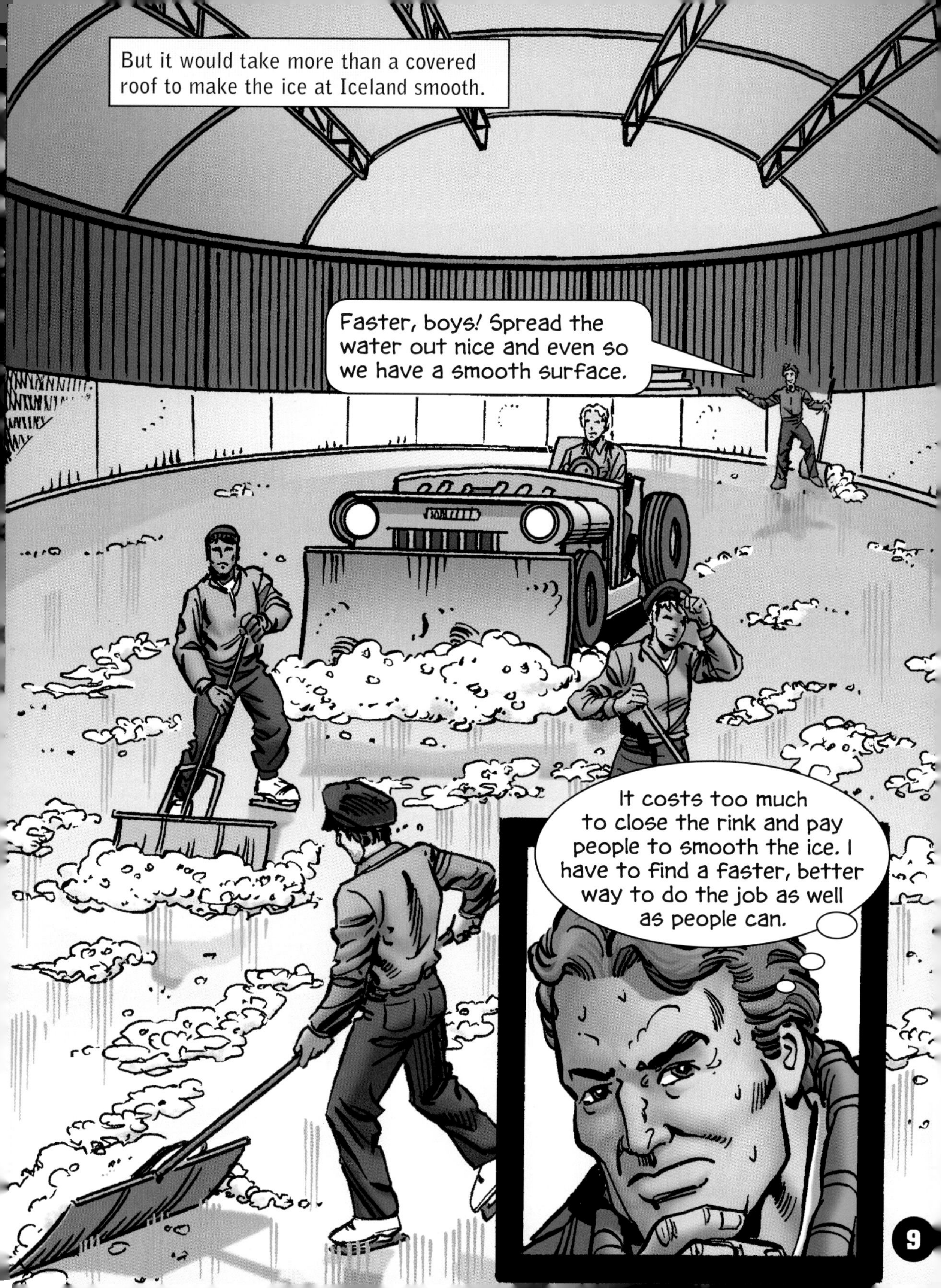

But it would take more than a covered roof to make the ice at Iceland smooth.
Faster, boys! Spread the water out nice and even so we have a smooth surface.
It costs too much to close the rink and pay people to smooth the ice. I have to find a faster, better way to do the job as well as people can.

Chapter 2
THE MODEL A

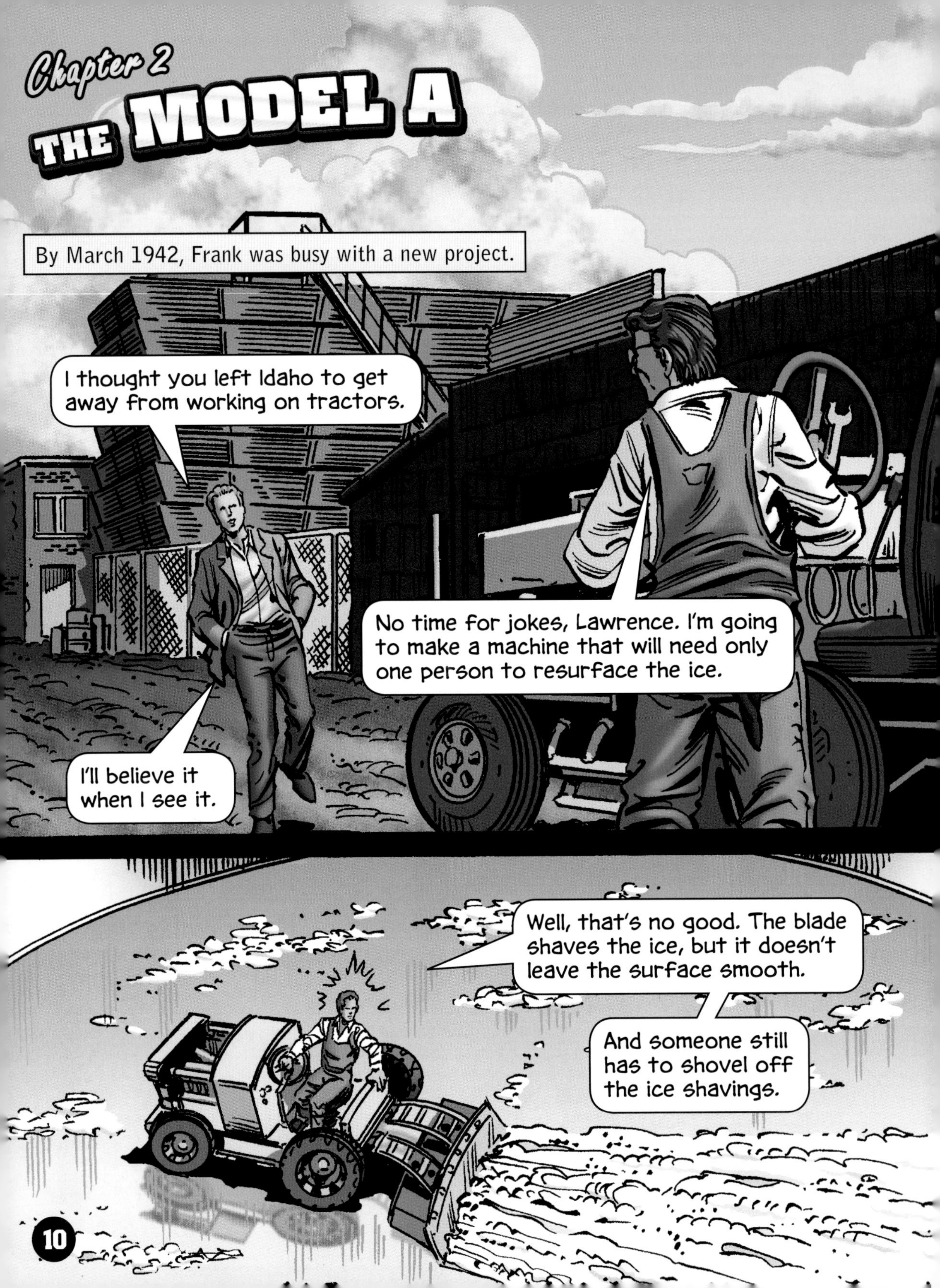
By March 1942, Frank was busy with a new project.
I thought you left Idaho to get away from working on tractors.
No time for jokes, Lawrence. I'm going to make a machine that will need only one person to resurface the ice.
I'll believe it when I see it.
Well, that's no good. The blade shaves the ice, but it doesn't leave the surface smooth.
And someone still has to shovel off the ice shavings.

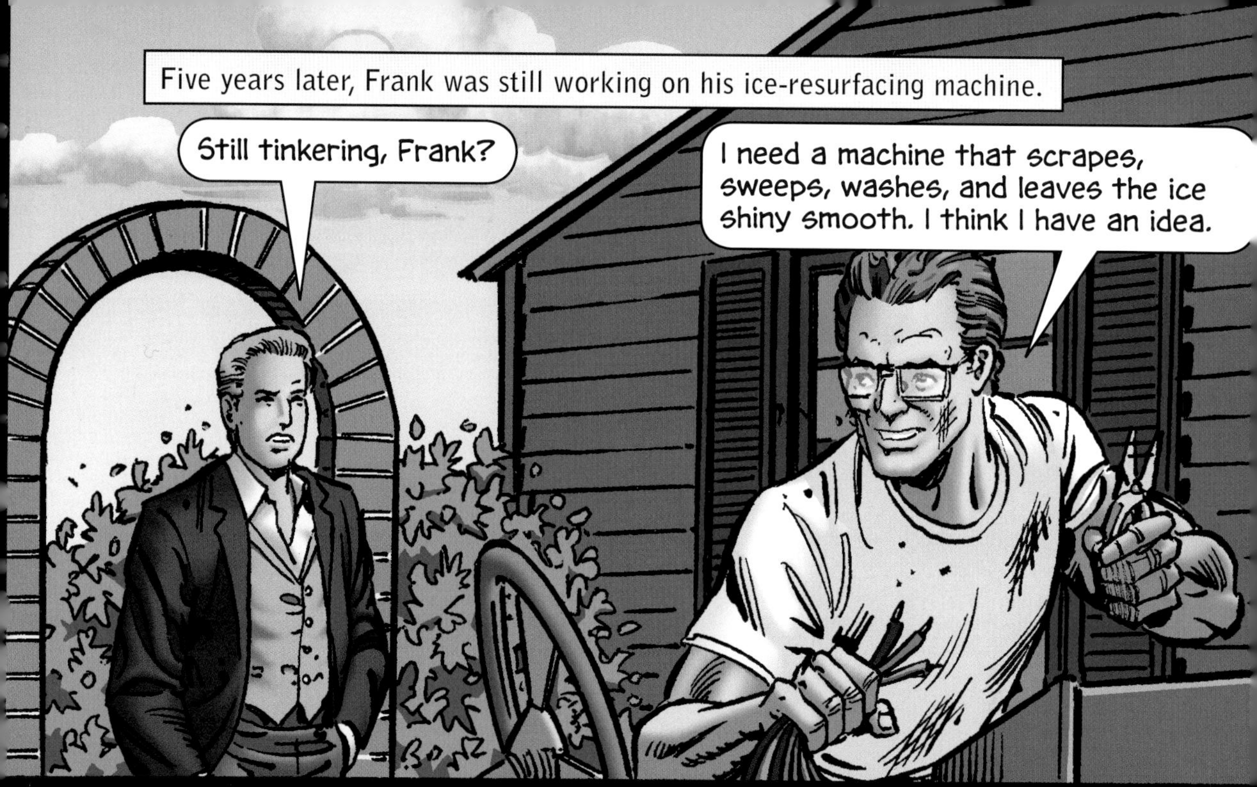
Five years later, Frank was still working on his ice-resurfacing machine.
Still tinkering, Frank?
I need a machine that scrapes, sweeps, washes, and leaves the ice shiny smooth. I think I have an idea.

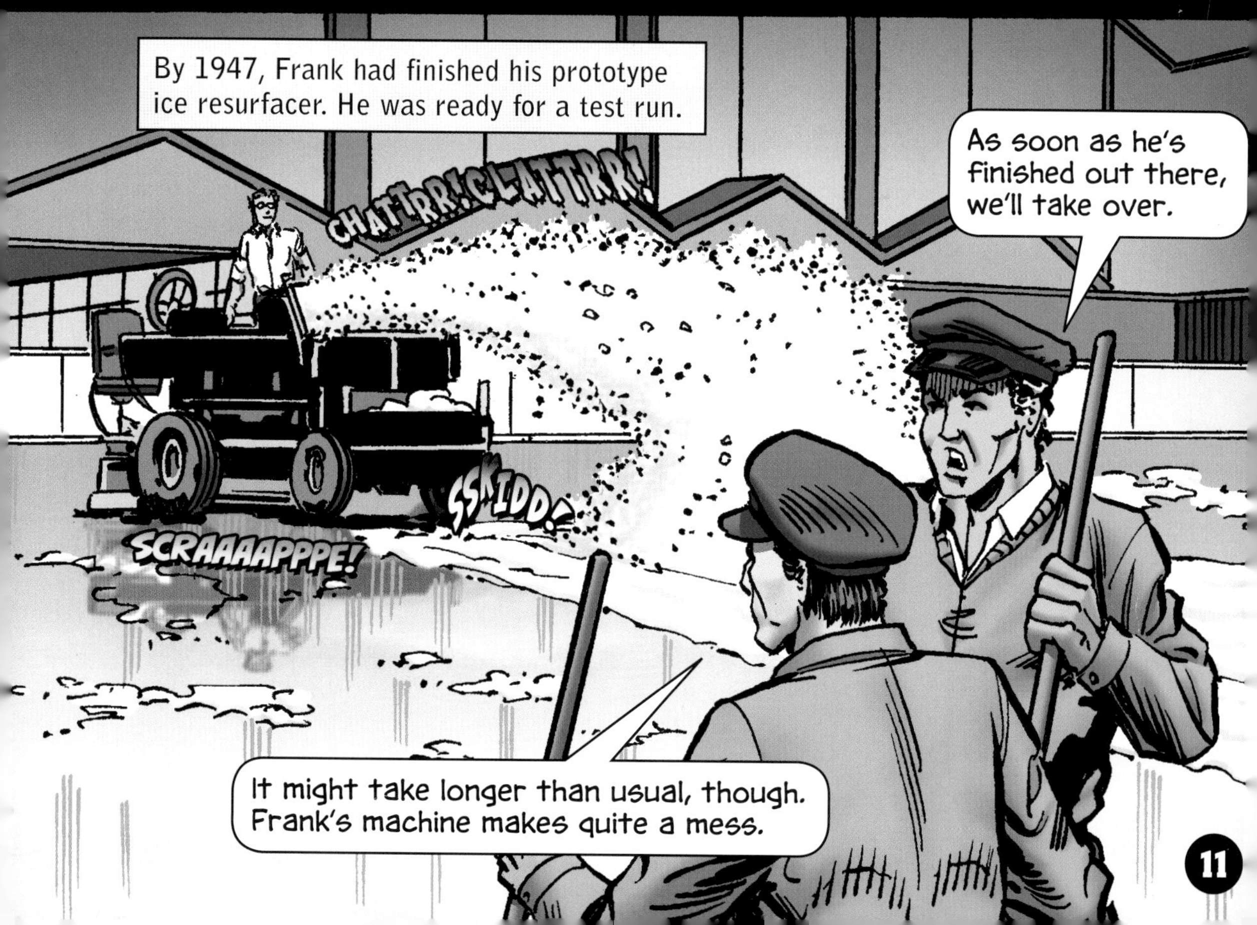
By 1947, Frank had finished his prototype ice resurfacer. He was ready for a test run.
CHATTRR!CLATTRR!
SSKIDD!
SCRAAAAPPPE!
As soon as he's finished out there, we'll take over.
It might take longer than usual, though. Frank's machine makes quite a mess.

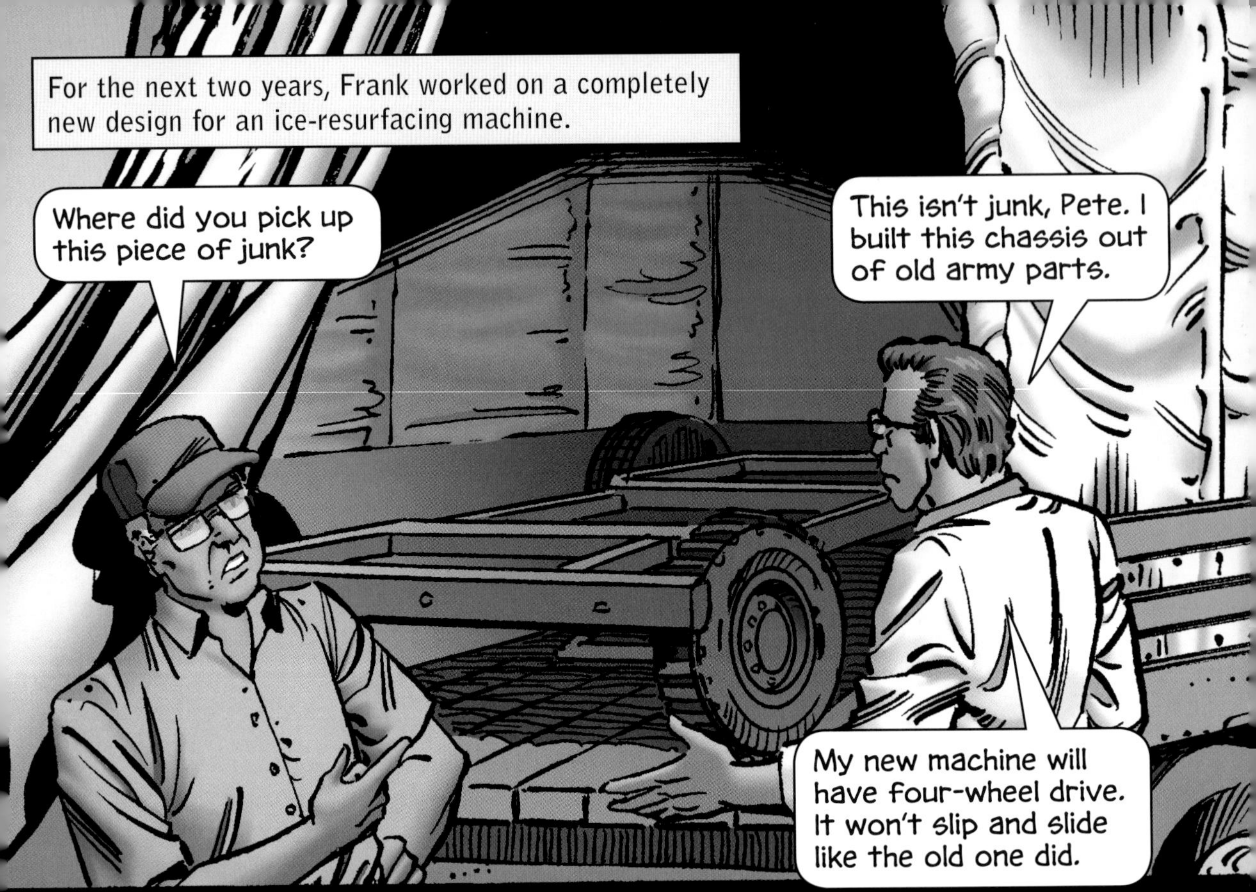
For the next two years, Frank worked on a completely new design for an ice-resurfacing machine.
Where did you pick up this piece of junk?
This isn't junk, Pete. I built this chassis out of old army parts.
My new machine will have four-wheel drive. It won't slip and slide like the old one did.

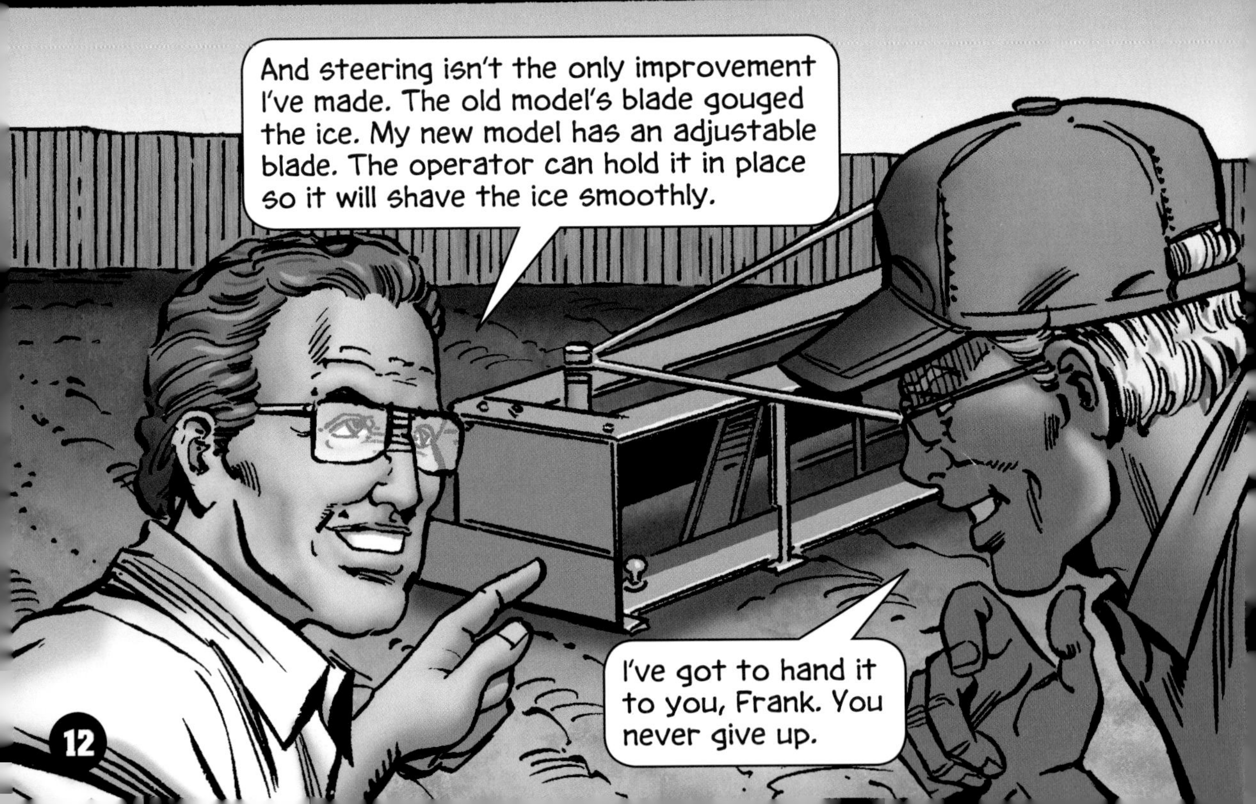
And steering isn't the only improvement I've made. The old model's blade gouged the ice. My new model has an adjustable blade. The operator can hold it in place so it will shave the ice smoothly.
I've got to hand it to you, Frank. You never give up.

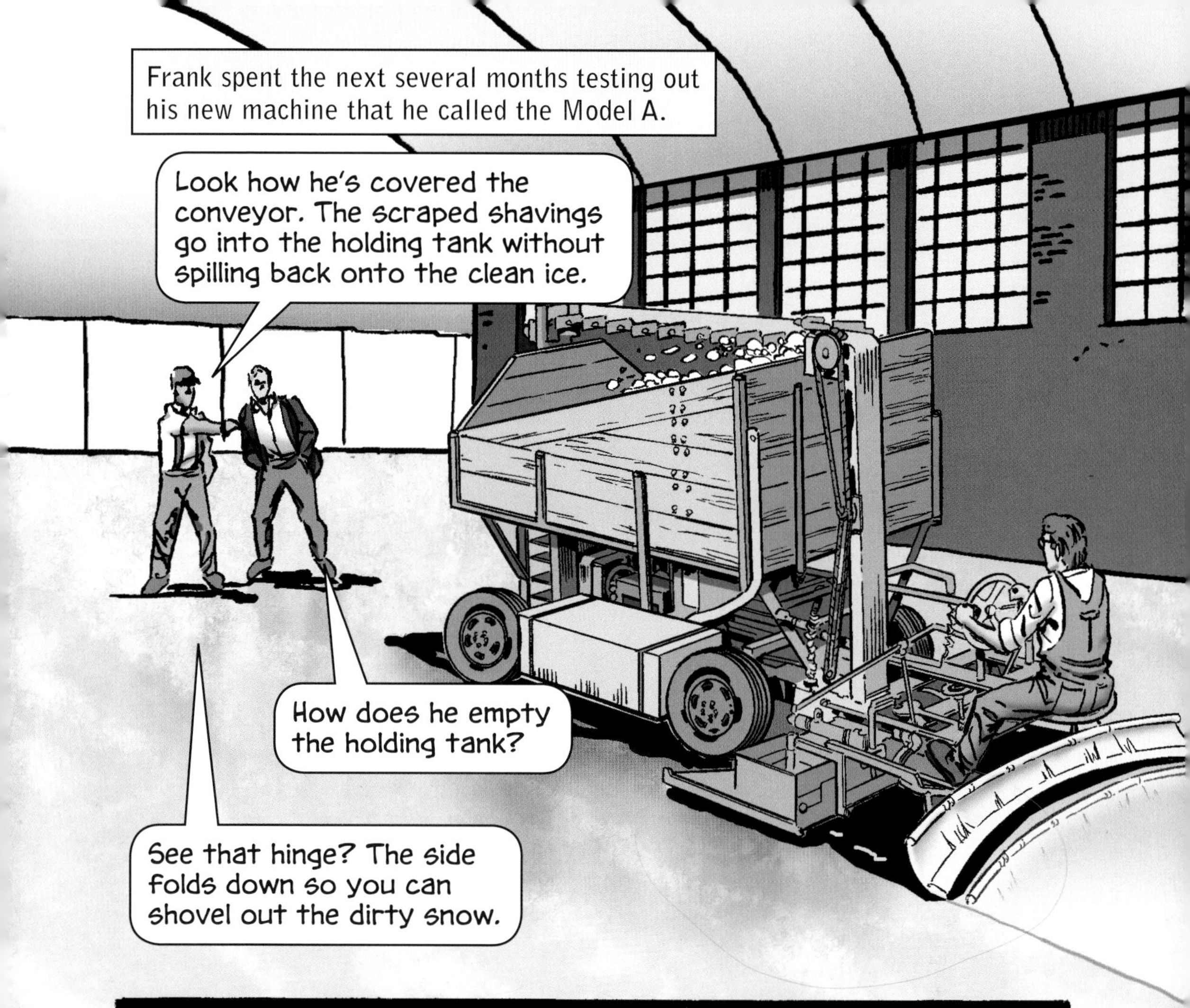
Frank spent the next several months testing out his new machine that he called the Model A.
Look how he's covered the conveyor. The scraped shavings go into the holding tank without spilling back onto the clean ice.
How does he empty the holding tank?
See that hinge? The side folds down so you can shovel out the dirty snow.

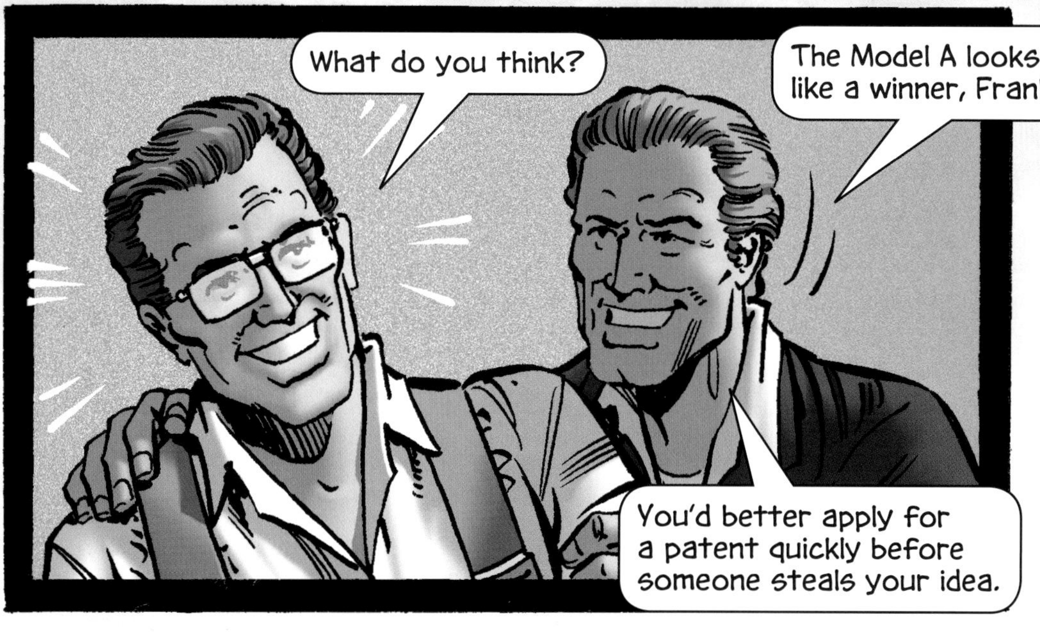
What do you think?
The Model A looks like a winner, Frank!
You'd better apply for a patent quickly before someone steals your idea.

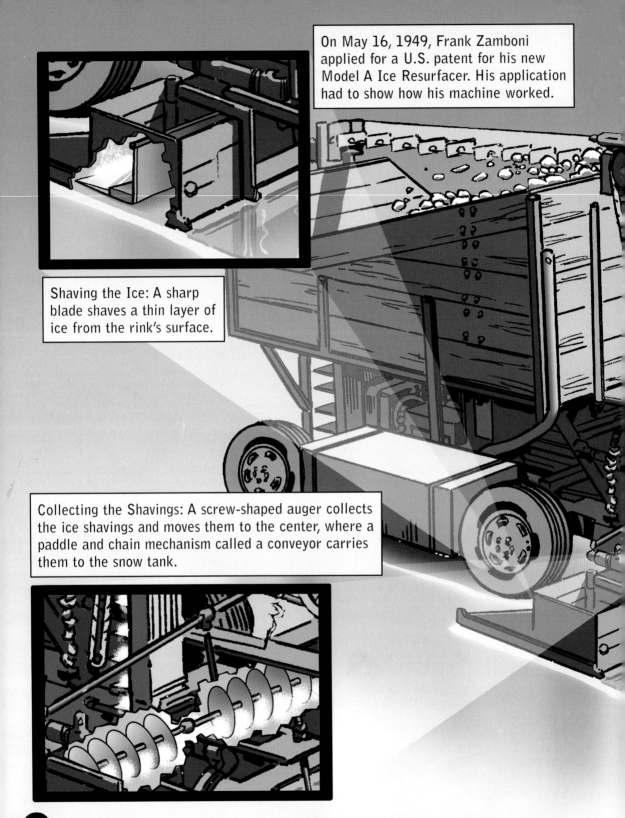

On May 16, 1949, Frank Zamboni applied for a U.S. patent for his new Model A Ice Resurfacer. His application had to show how his machine worked.

Shaving the Ice: A sharp blade shaves a thin layer of ice from the rink's surface.

Collecting the Shavings: A screw-shaped auger collects the ice shavings and moves them to the center, where a paddle and chain mechanism called a conveyor carries them to the snow tank.

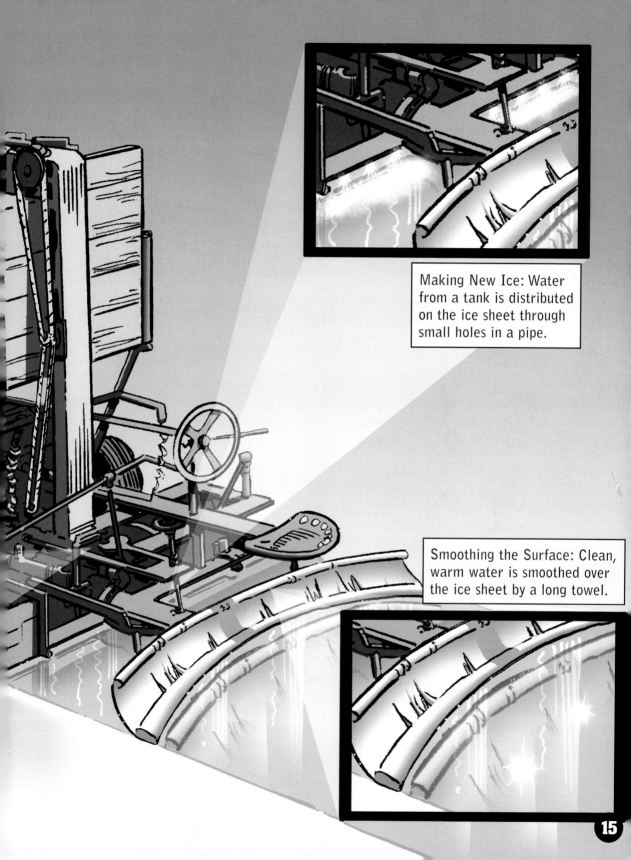

Making New Ice: Water from a tank is distributed on the ice sheet through small holes in a pipe.

Smoothing the Surface: Clean, warm water is smoothed over the ice sheet by a long towel.

Chapter 3
THE ZAMBONI COMPANY

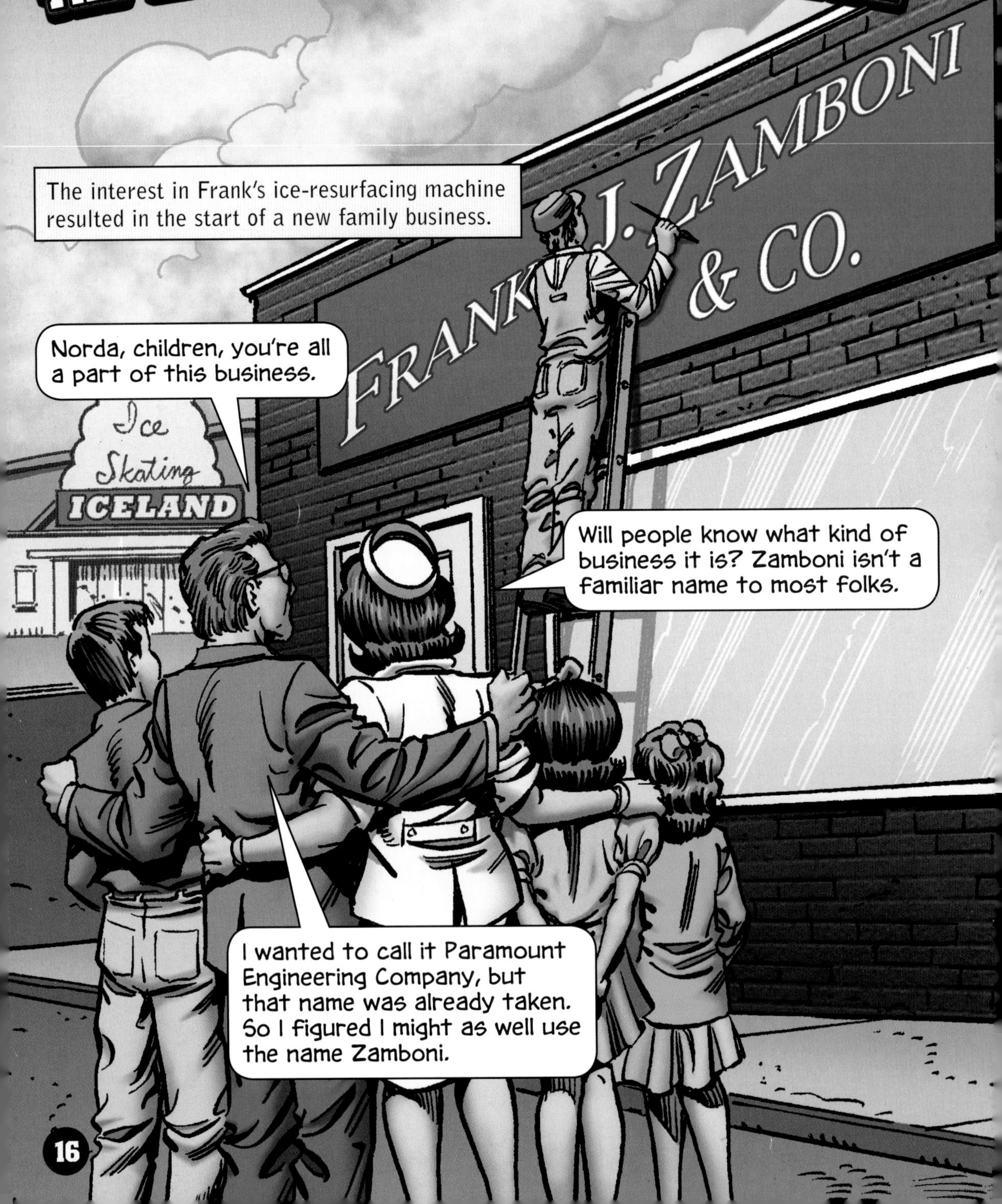

The interest in Frank's ice-resurfacing machine resulted in the start of a new family business.
FRANK J. ZAMBONI & CO.
Norda, children, you're all a part of this business.
Ice Skating
ICELAND
Will people know what kind of business it is? Zamboni isn't a familiar name to most folks.
I wanted to call it Paramount Engineering Company, but that name was already taken. So I figured I might as well use the name Zamboni.

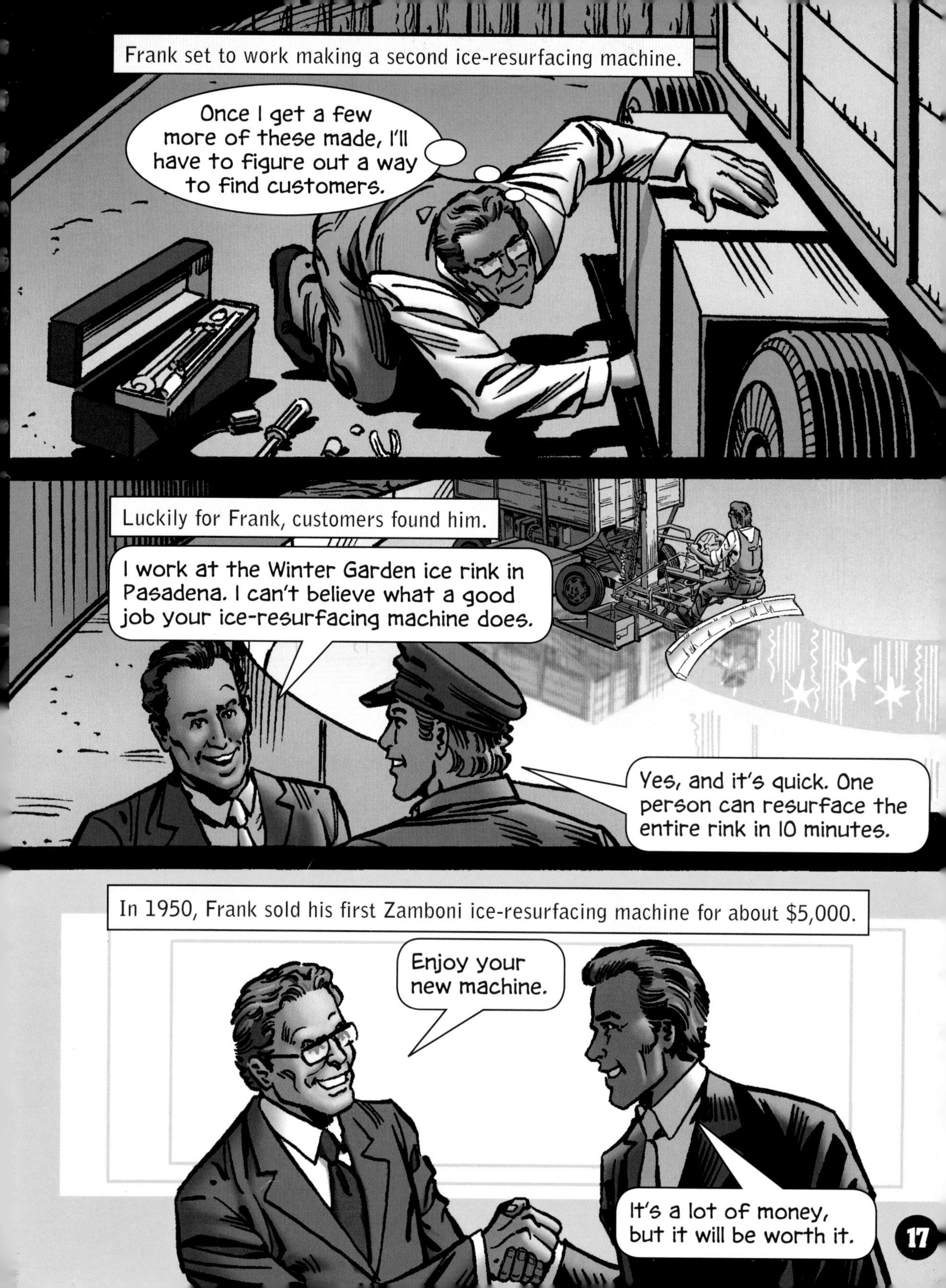

Frank set to work making a second ice-resurfacing machine.
Once I get a few more of these made, I'll have to figure out a way to find customers.
Luckily for Frank, customers found him.
I work at the Winter Garden ice rink in Pasadena. I can't believe what a good job your ice-resurfacing machine does.
Yes, and it's quick. One person can resurface the entire rink in 10 minutes.
In 1950, Frank sold his first Zamboni ice-resurfacing machine for about $5,000.
Enjoy your new machine.
It's a lot of money, but it will be worth it.

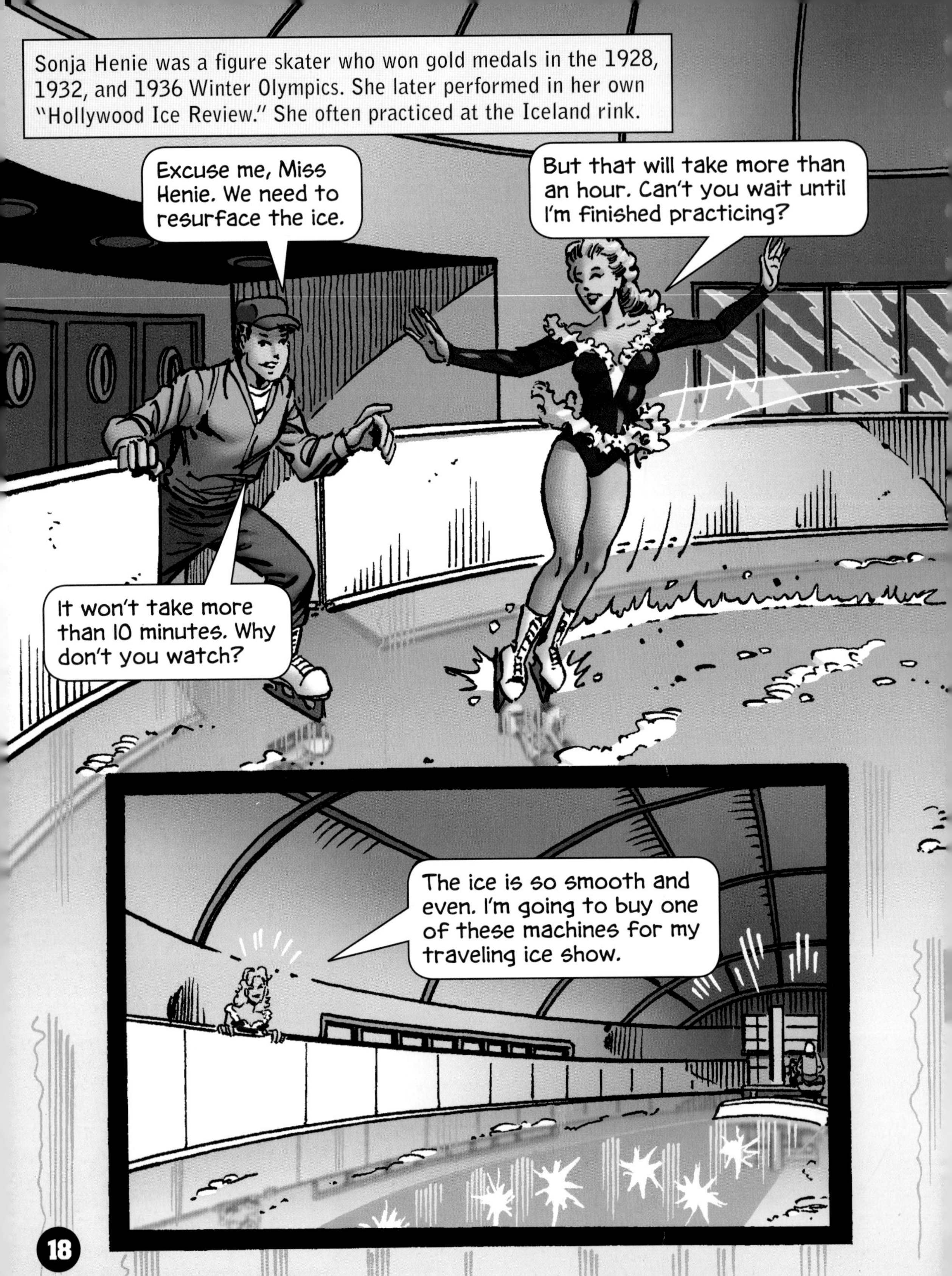
Sonja Henie was a figure skater who won gold medals in the 1928, 1932, and 1936 Winter Olympics. She later performed in her own "Hollywood Ice Review." She often practiced at the Iceland rink.
Excuse me, Miss Henie. We need to resurface the ice.
But that will take more than an hour. Can't you wait until I'm finished practicing?
It won't take more than 10 minutes. Why don't you watch?
The ice is so smooth and even. I'm going to buy one of these machines for my traveling ice show.

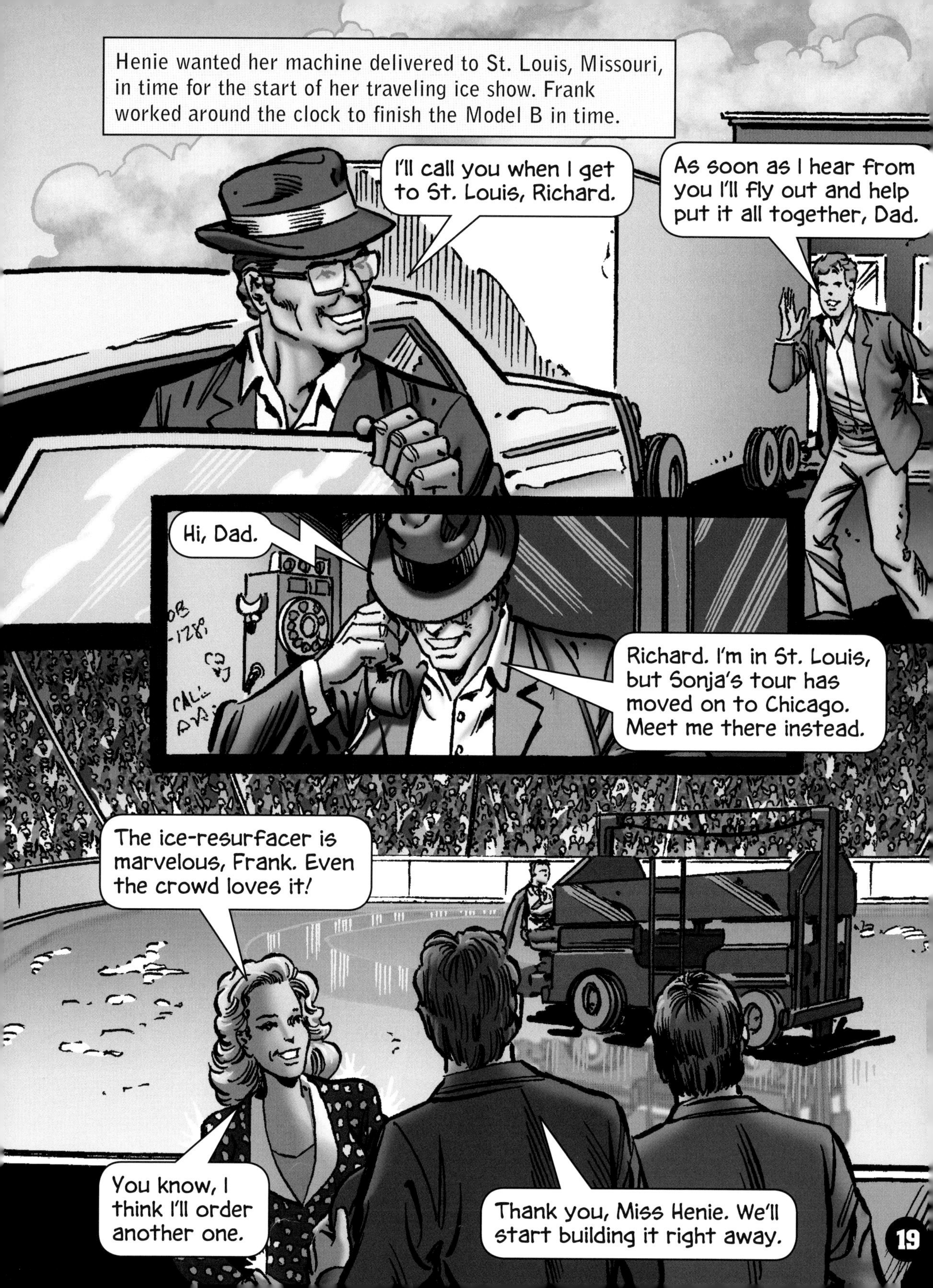

Henie wanted her machine delivered to St. Louis, Missouri, in time for the start of her traveling ice show. Frank worked around the clock to finish the Model B in time.
I'll call you when I get to St. Louis, Richard.
As soon as I hear from you I'll fly out and help put it all together, Dad.
Hi, Dad.
Richard. I'm in St. Louis, but Sonja's tour has moved on to Chicago. Meet me there instead.
The ice-resurfacer is marvelous, Frank. Even the crowd loves it!
You know, I think I'll order another one.
Thank you, Miss Henie. We'll start building it right away.

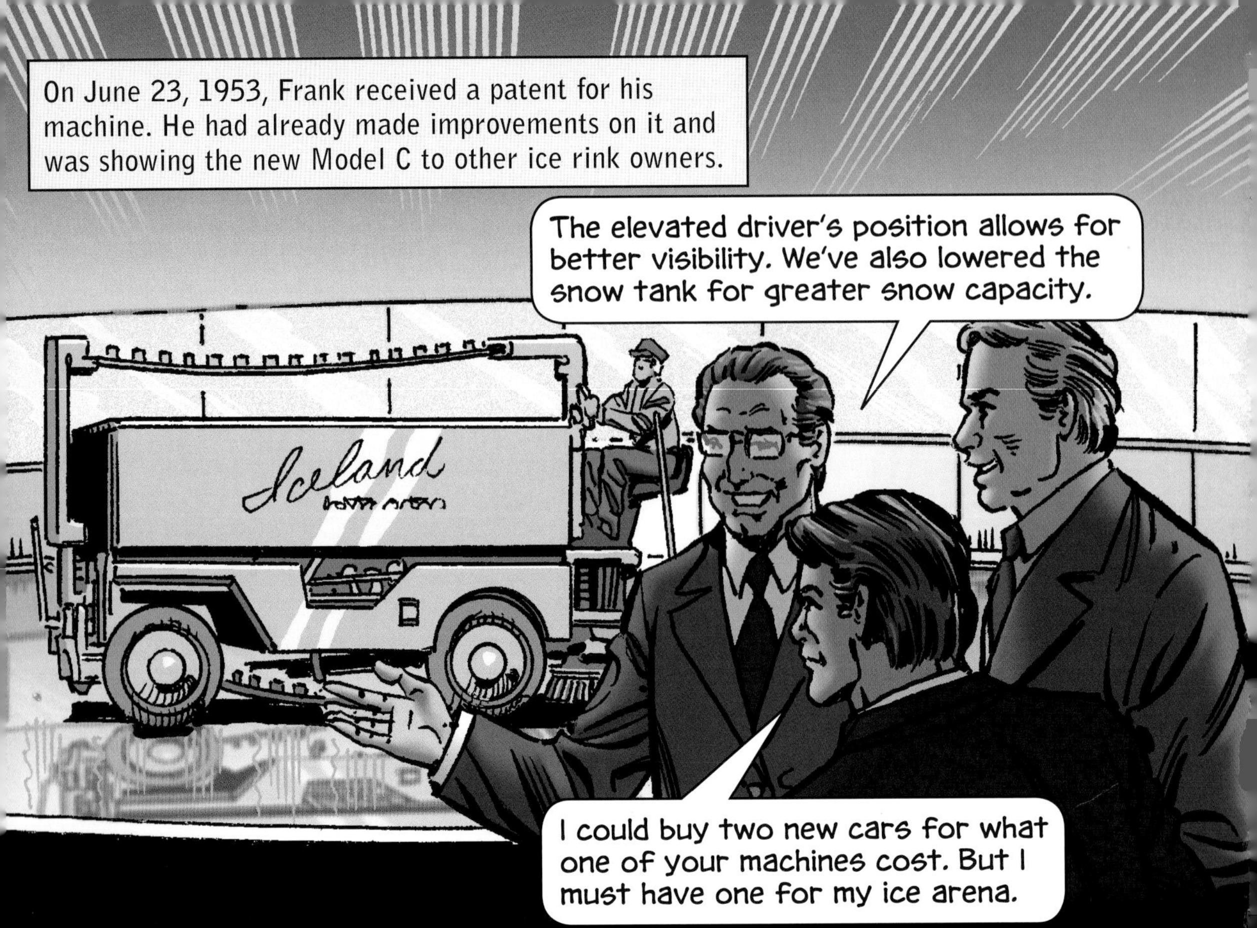
On June 23, 1953, Frank received a patent for his machine. He had already made improvements on it and was showing the new Model C to other ice rink owners.
The elevated driver's position allows for better visibility. We've also lowered the snow tank for greater snow capacity.
Iceland
I could buy two new cars for what one of your machines cost. But I must have one for my ice arena.

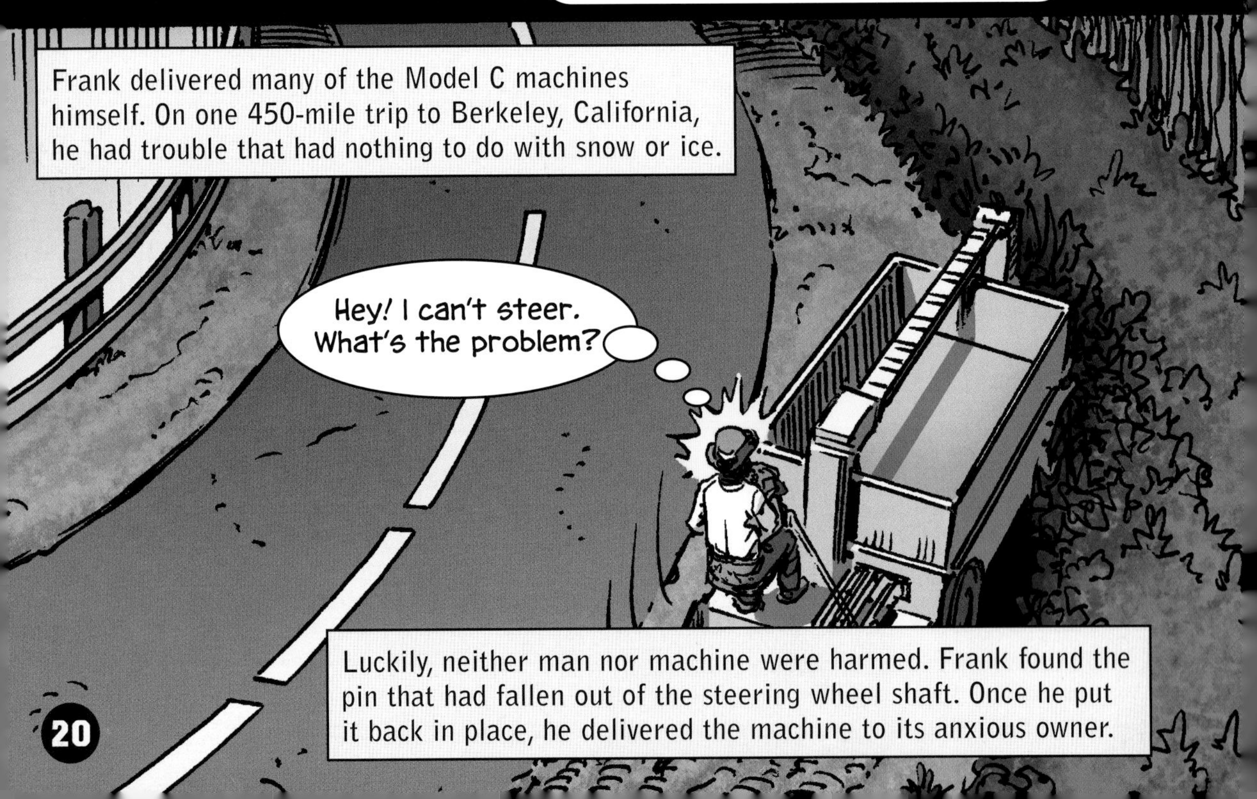
Frank delivered many of the Model C machines himself. On one 450-mile trip to Berkeley, California, he had trouble that had nothing to do with snow or ice.
Hey! I can't steer. What's the problem?
Luckily, neither man nor machine were harmed. Frank found the pin that had fallen out of the steering wheel shaft. Once he put it back in place, he delivered the machine to its anxious owner.

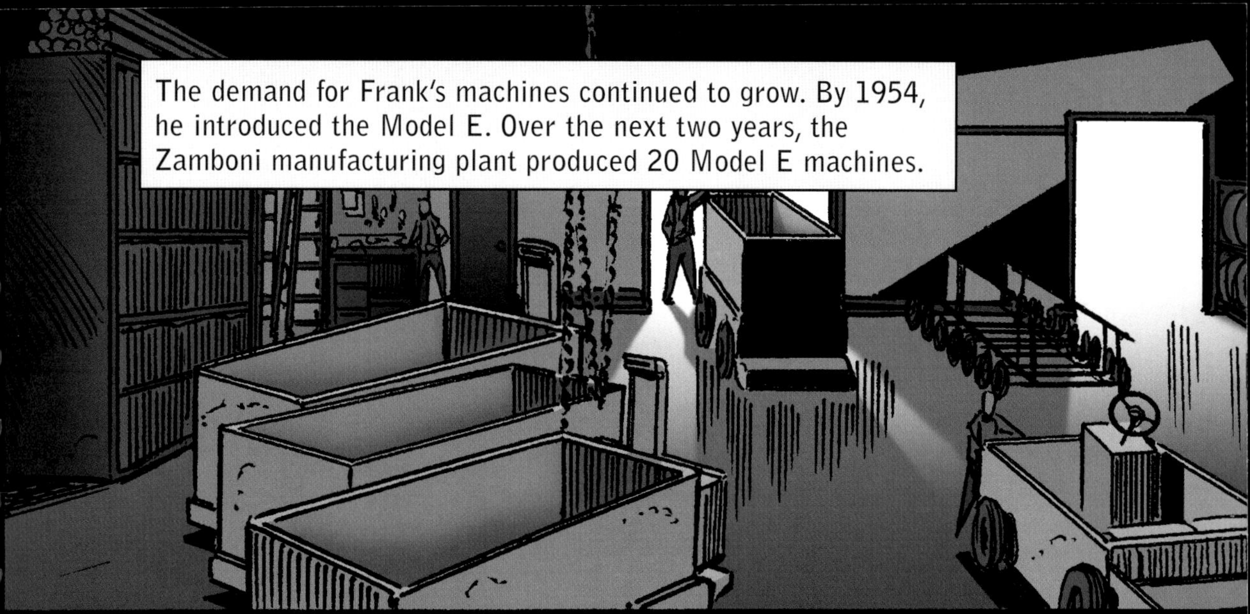

The demand for Frank's machines continued to grow. By 1954, he introduced the Model E. Over the next two years, the Zamboni manufacturing plant produced 20 Model E machines.

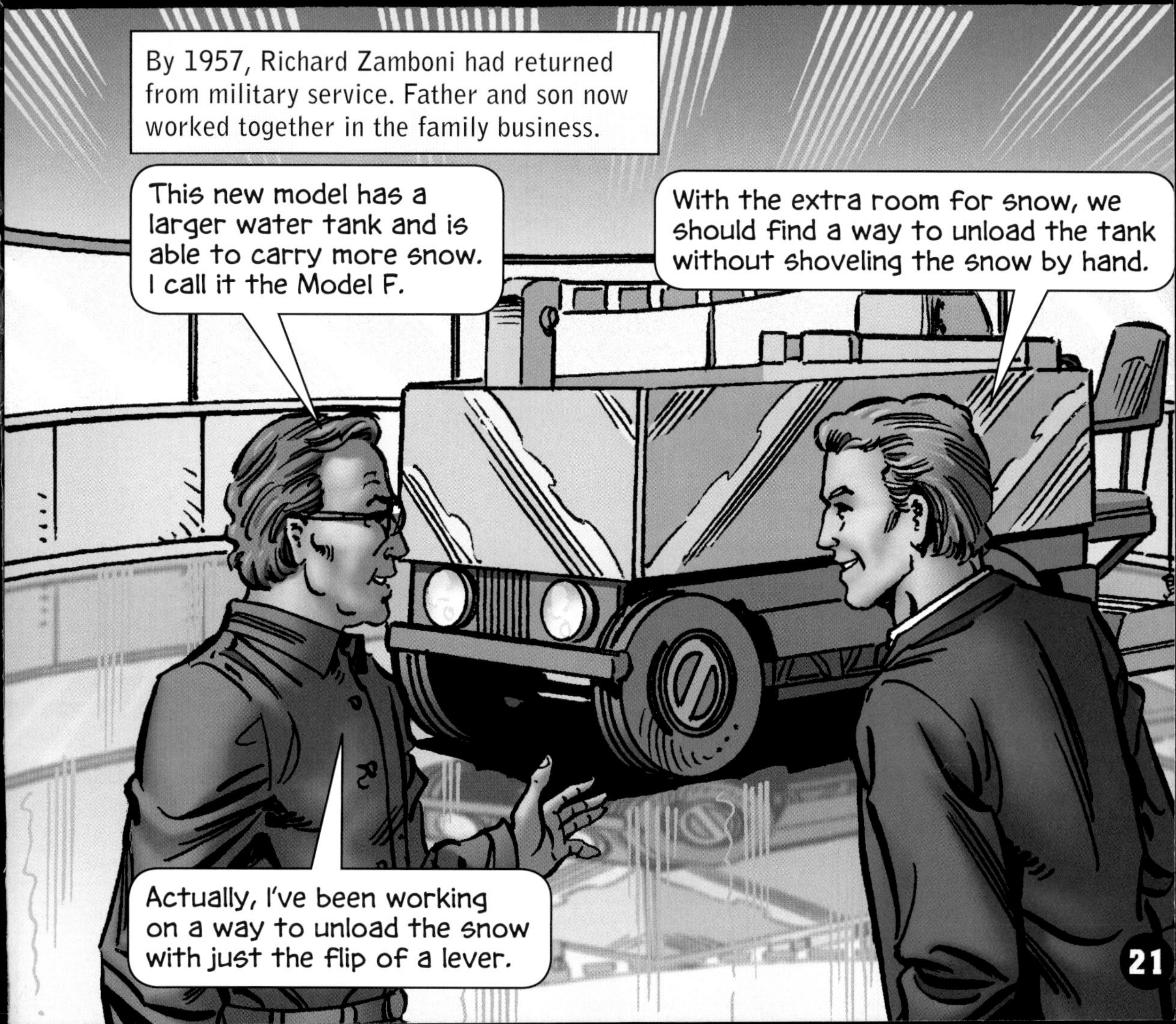

By 1957, Richard Zamboni had returned from military service. Father and son now worked together in the family business.
This new model has a larger water tank and is able to carry more snow. I call it the Model F.
With the extra room for snow, we should find a way to unload the tank without shoveling the snow by hand.
Actually, I've been working on a way to unload the snow with just the flip of a lever.

Chapter 4
ICING ON THE RINK

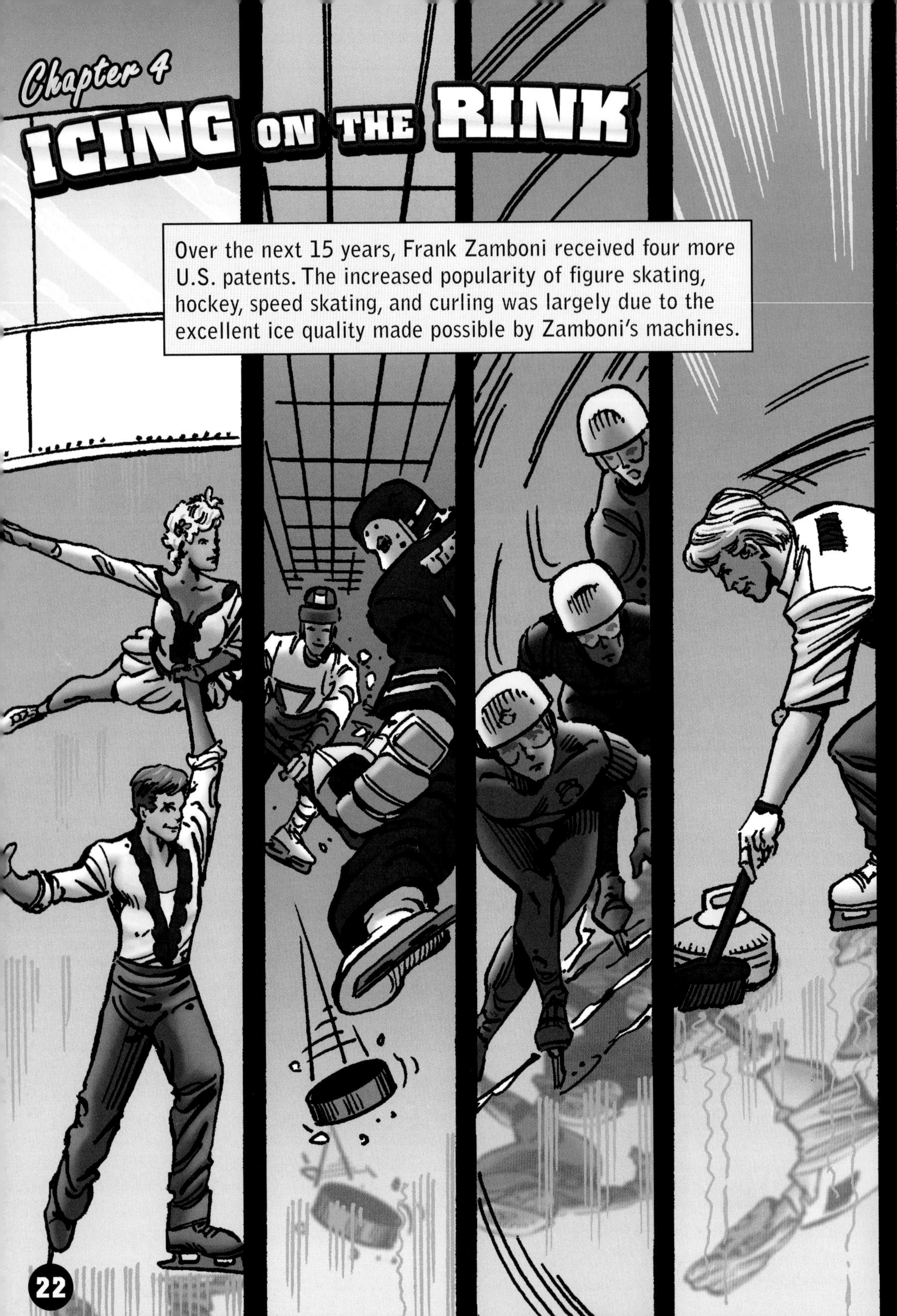
Over the next 15 years, Frank Zamboni received four more U.S. patents. The increased popularity of figure skating, hockey, speed skating, and curling was largely due to the excellent ice quality made possible by Zamboni's machines.

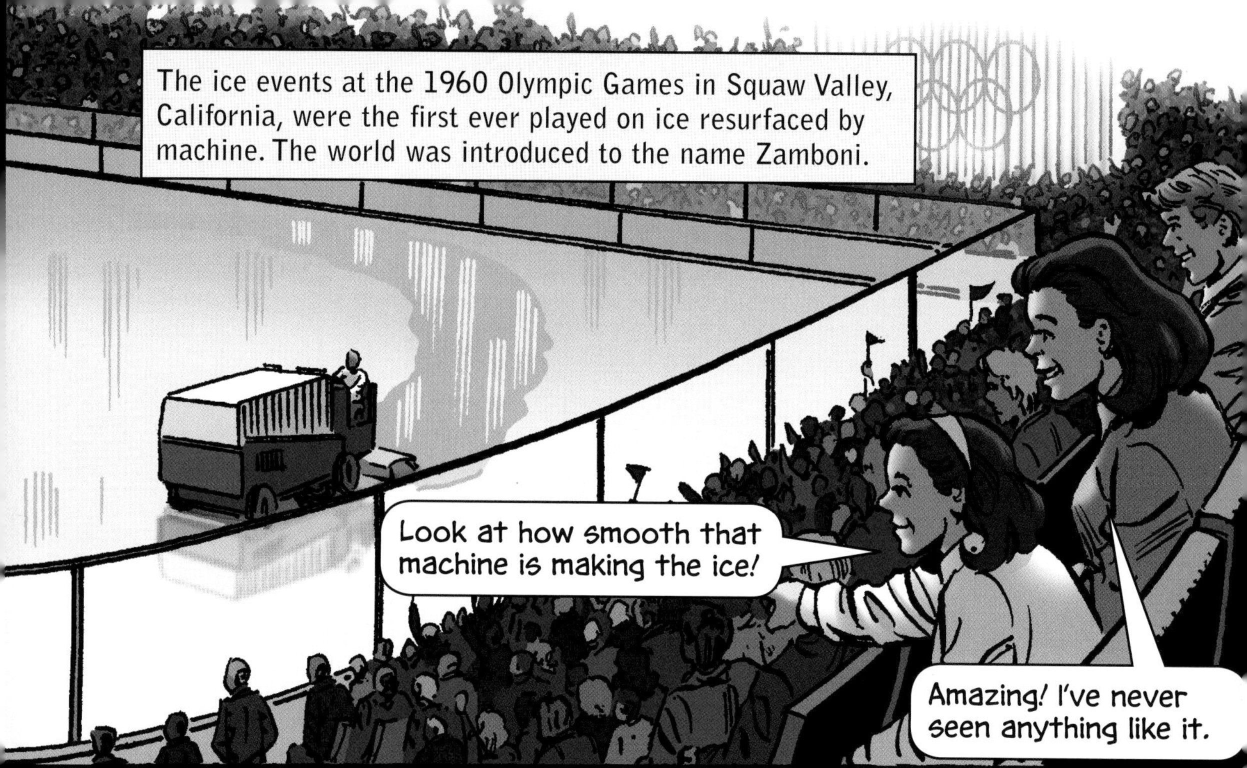
The ice events at the 1960 Olympic Games in Squaw Valley, California, were the first ever played on ice resurfaced by machine. The world was introduced to the name Zamboni.
Look at how smooth that machine is making the ice!
Amazing! I've never seen anything like it.

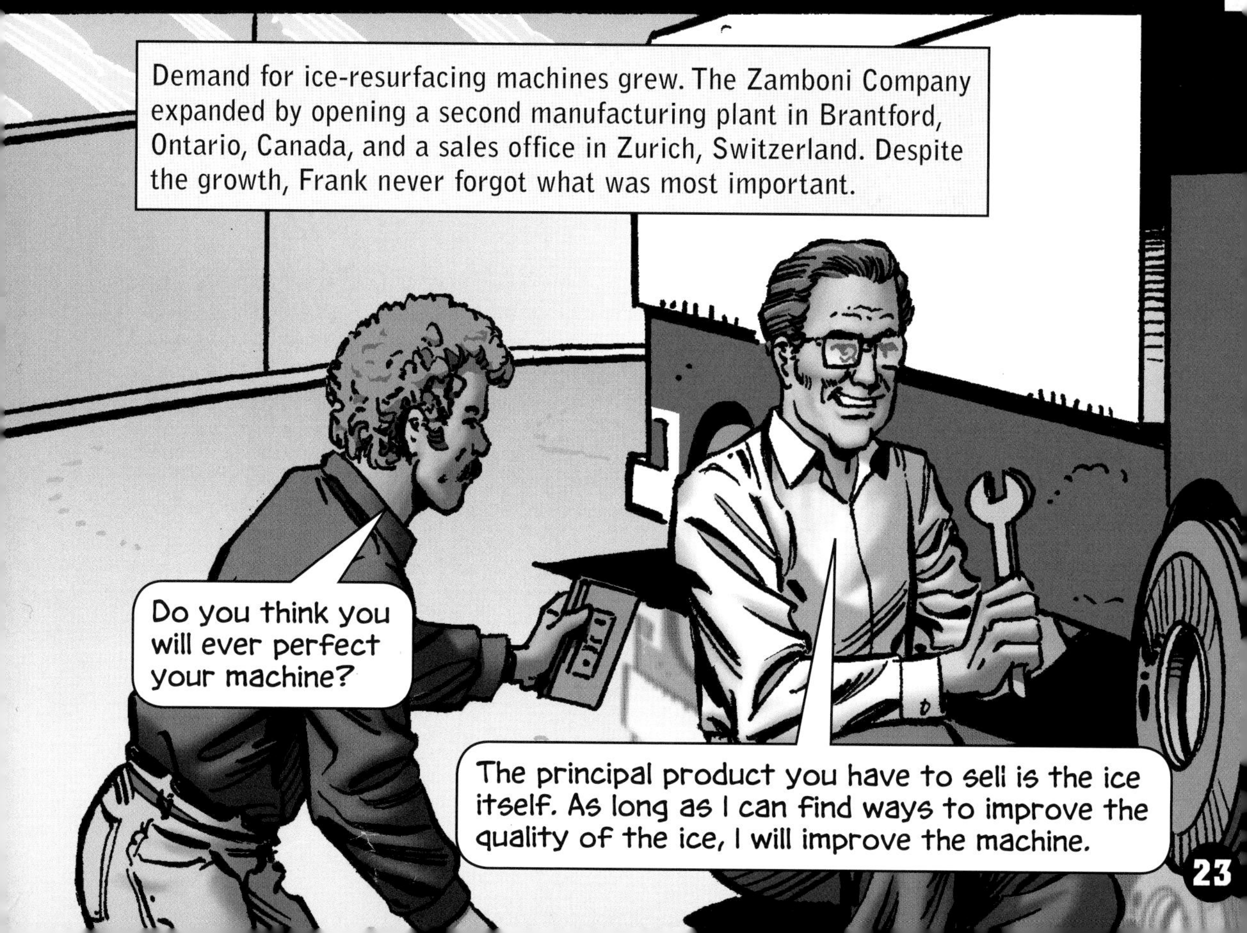
Demand for ice-resurfacing machines grew. The Zamboni Company expanded by opening a second manufacturing plant in Brantford, Ontario, Canada, and a sales office in Zurich, Switzerland. Despite the growth, Frank never forgot what was most important.
Do you think you will ever perfect your machine?
The principal product you have to sell is the ice itself. As long as I can find ways to improve the quality of the ice, I will improve the machine.

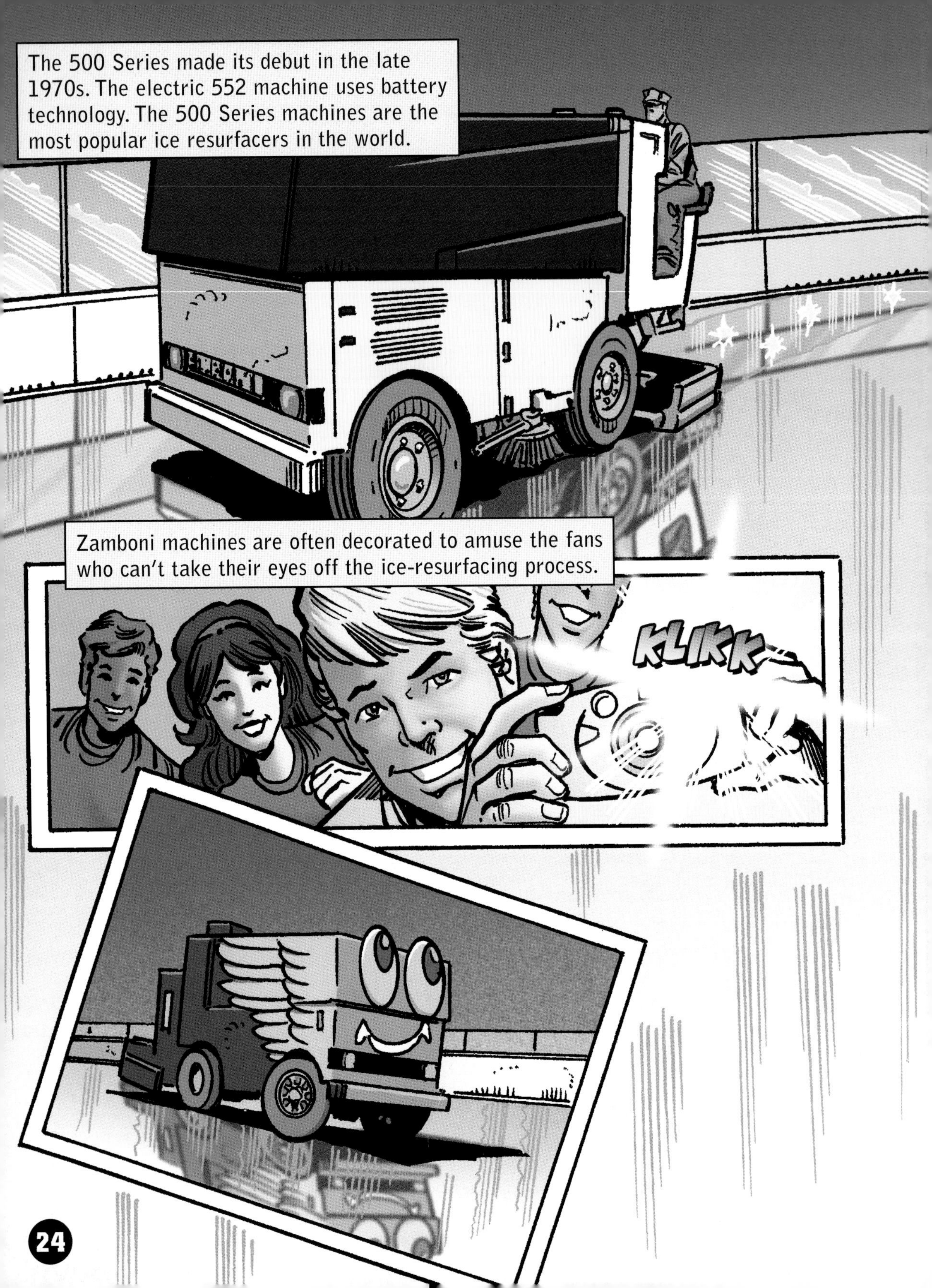
The 500 Series made its debut in the late 1970s. The electric 552 machine uses battery technology. The 500 Series machines are the most popular ice resurfacers in the world.
Zamboni machines are often decorated to amuse the fans who can't take their eyes off the ice-resurfacing process.
KLIKK

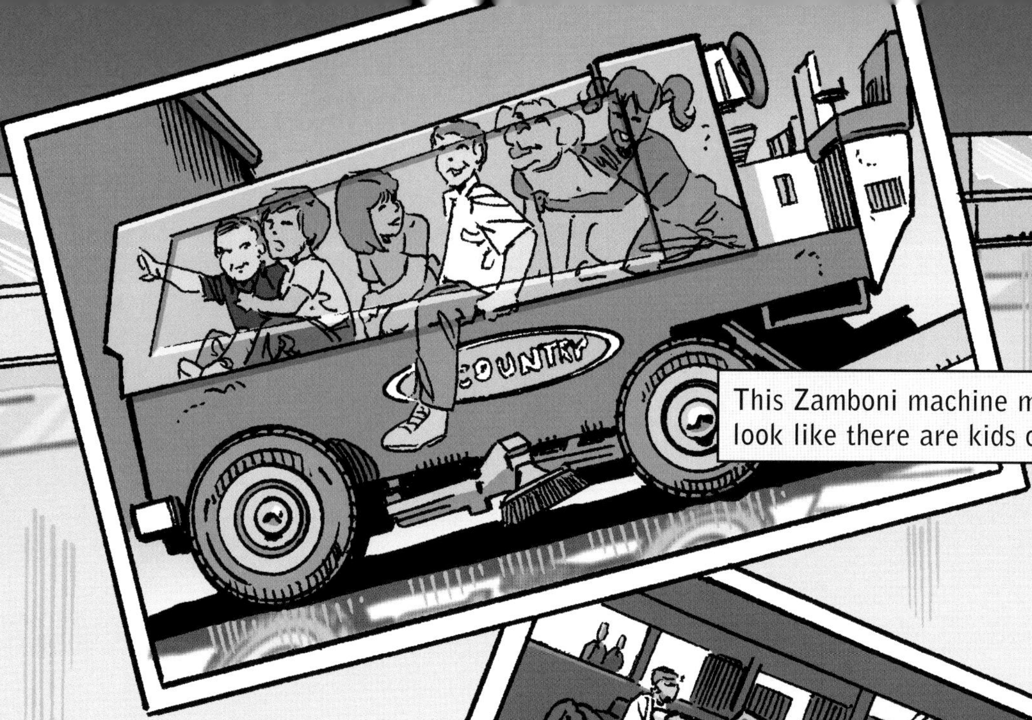
COUNTRY

This Zamboni machine makes it look like there are kids on board.

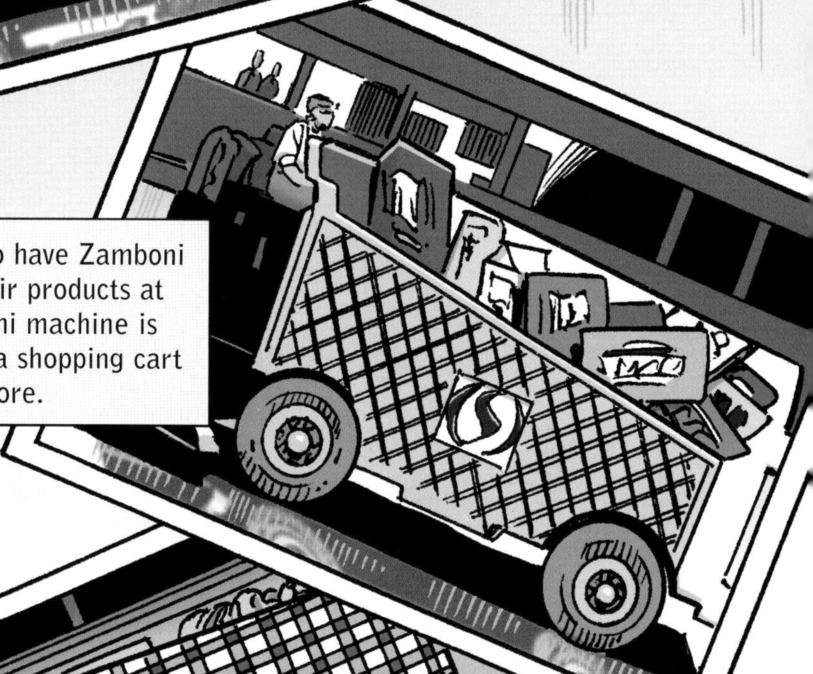

Some businesses pay to have Zamboni machines advertise their products at ice events. This Zamboni machine is decorated to look like a shopping cart from a local grocery store.

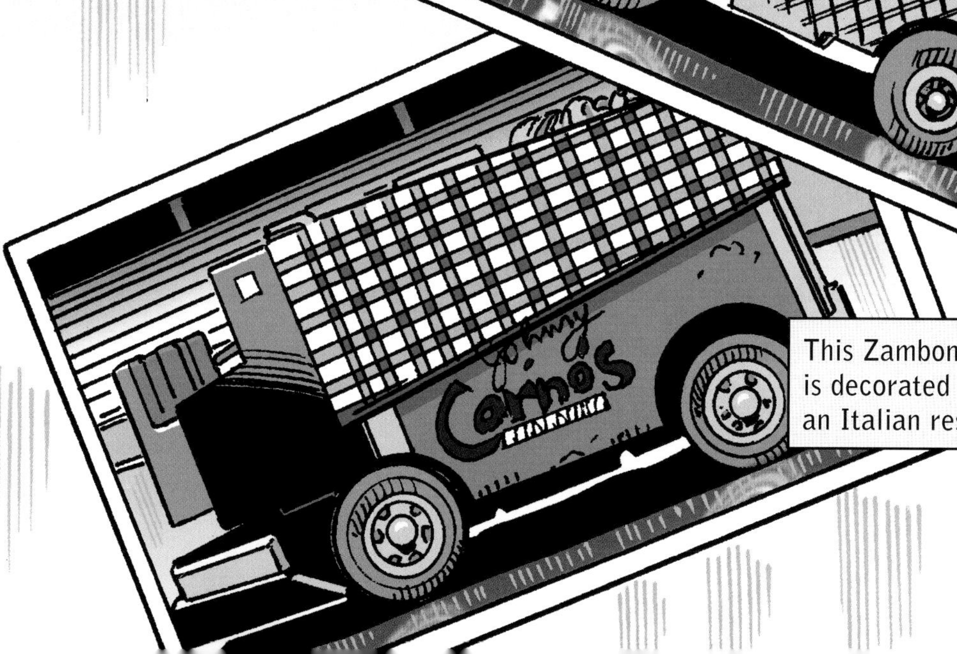

This Zamboni machine is decorated to advertise an Italian restaurant.

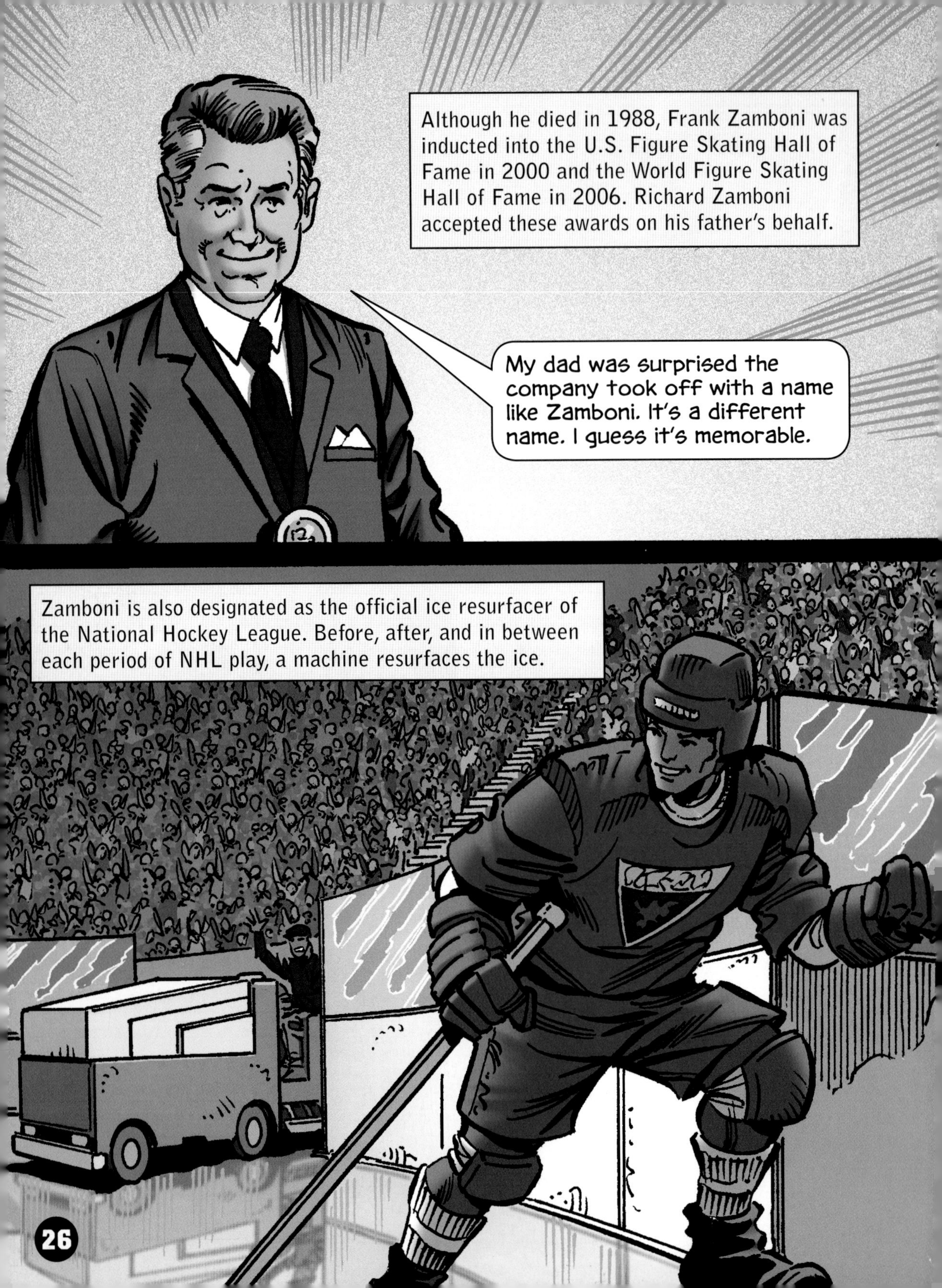
Although he died in 1988, Frank Zamboni was inducted into the U.S. Figure Skating Hall of Fame in 2000 and the World Figure Skating Hall of Fame in 2006. Richard Zamboni accepted these awards on his father's behalf.
My dad was surprised the company took off with a name like Zamboni. It's a different name. I guess it's memorable.
Zamboni is also designated as the official ice resurfacer of the National Hockey League. Before, after, and in between each period of NHL play, a machine resurfaces the ice.

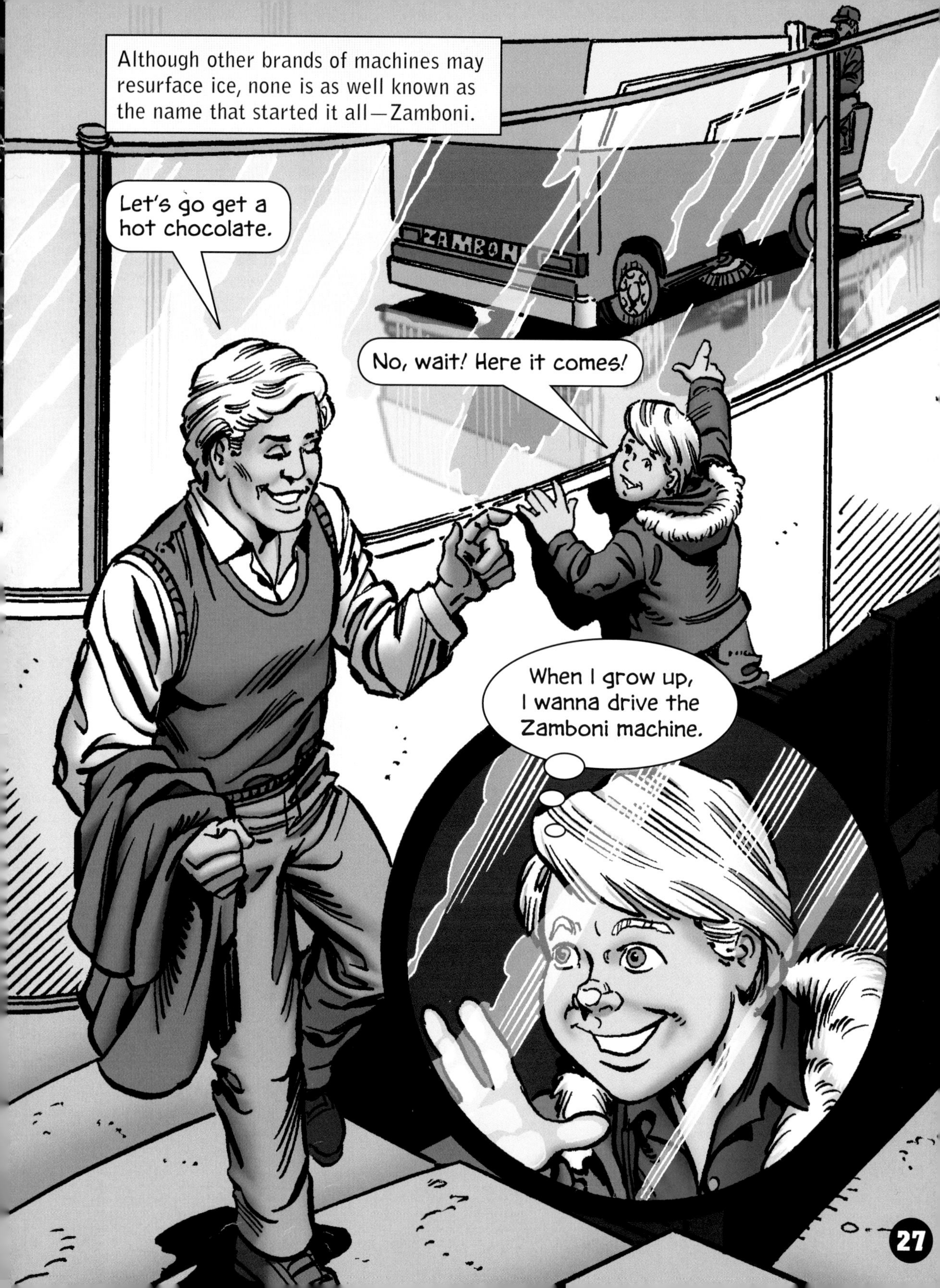
Although other brands of machines may resurface ice, none is as well known as the name that started it all—Zamboni.
Let's go get a hot chocolate.
ZAMBONI
No, wait! Here it comes!
When I grow up, I wanna drive the Zamboni machine.

MORE ABOUT FRANK ZAMBONI
and the Ice-Resurfacing Machine

Frank Zamboni was born January 16, 1901, in Eureka, Utah, south of Salt Lake City. He was raised on a farm in Idaho. He died July 27, 1988.

Frank left school at age 15 to help his father on the family farm. In 1920, the family sold the farm and moved to California. The family saved for a year to get enough money to send Frank to the Coyne Trade School in Chicago to learn the electrical business.

Before Frank invented the ice-resurfacing machine, the ice had to be resurfaced by hand. This process required three or four workers and took more than an hour to complete.

The first Zamboni Ice Resurfacing Machine, the Model A, was invented at Paramount Iceland in 1949. It was recently restored and today is fully operational.

Zamboni machines have a top speed of about 9 miles (14 kilometers) per hour.

Zamboni machines travel an average of 3 miles (4.8 kilometers) during each hockey game. On average, a Zamboni machine covers about 2,000 miles (3,200 kilometers) each year in the course of resurfacing.

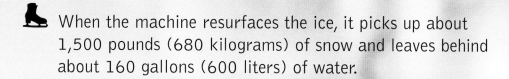 When the machine resurfaces the ice, it picks up about 1,500 pounds (680 kilograms) of snow and leaves behind about 160 gallons (600 liters) of water.

The blade on the Zamboni machine is designed especially for ice-resurfacing. It weighs 57 pounds (26 kilograms), is one-half inch (1.2 centimeters) thick, and is sharp enough to slice through thick stacks of paper.

Frank J. Zamboni & Co. is still a family-run business. Each plant employs about 30 people, and the machines are built year-round. Each Zamboni machine is hand-assembled, one at a time. Customers may wait as long as eight months to receive their machine after ordering.

Frank Zamboni is still gaining recognition for his invention. In addition to his other honors, he was inducted into the National Inventors Hall of Fame in May 2007.

GLOSSARY

adjustable (uh-JUHS-tuh-buhl)—able to be moved or changed slightly

chassis (CHASS-ee)—the frame on which a vehicle is built

conveyor belt (kuhn-VAY-ur BELT)—a moving belt that carries objects from one place to another

induct (in-DUHKT)—to formally admit someone into a position or place of honor

patent (PAT-uhnt)—a legal document that gives an inventor the right to make, use, or sell an invention for a set period of years

technology (tek-NOL-uh-jee)—the use of science and engineering to do practical things

INTERNET SITES

FactHound offers a safe, fun way to find Internet sites related to this book. All of the sites on FactHound have been researched by our staff.

Here's how:
1. Visit *www.facthound.com*
2. Choose your grade level.
3. Type in this book ID **1429601477** for age-appropriate sites. You may also browse subjects by clicking on letters, or by clicking on pictures and words.
4. Click on the **Fetch It** button.

FactHound will fetch the best sites for you!

READ MORE

Devantier, Alecia T. *Extraordinary Jobs in Sports.* Extraordinary Jobs. New York: Ferguson, 2007.

Dregni, Eric. *Zamboni: The Coolest Machines on Ice.* St. Paul, Minn.: Voyageur Press, 2006.

Napier, Matt. *Z is for Zamboni: A Hockey Alphabet.* Chelsea, Mich.: Sleeping Bear Press, 2002.

Thomas, Keltie. *How Hockey Works.* Toronto: Maple Tree Press, 2006.

BIBLIOGRAPHY

The World Figure Skating Hall of Fame—Frank J. Zamboni. http://www.worldskatingmuseum.org/RichardZamboni-2006WorldHallofFame.htm.

Frank J. Zamboni & Co. Inc—The Zamboni Story. http://www.zamboni.com/story/story.html.

Zane, D. B. *The Great Zamboni.* Cypress, Calif.: Dizon, 1998.

INDEX